Access My eLab LEAP 1

leap 1
READING AND WRITING

DR. KEN BEATTY

Pearson   GSE

TO REGISTER

❶ Go to **http://mybookshelf.pearsonerpi.com**

❷ Follow the instructions. When asked for your access code, please type the code provided underneath the blue sticker.

❸ To access **My eLab** at any time, go to http://mybookshelf.pearsonerpi.com. **Bookmark this page for quicker access.**

Access to My eLab is valid for 12 months from the date of registration.

WARNING! This book CANNOT BE RETURNED if the access code has been uncovered.

Note: Once you have registered, you will need to join your online class. Ask your teacher to provide you with the class ID.

TEACHER Access Code

To obtain an access code for My eLab, please contact your Pearson ELT consultant.

1 800 263-3678, ext. 2
pearsonerpi.com/help

W138347 (A38395)

1460

leap 1

DR. KEN BEATTY

READING
AND **WRITING**

Pearson

Product Owner
Stephan Leduc

Managing Editor
Sharnee Chait

Project Editor
Linda Barton

Proofreader
Sheryl Curtis

Rights and Permissions Coordinator
Aude Maggiori

Text Rights and Permissions
Rachel Irwin

Art Director
Hélène Cousineau

Graphic Design Coordinator
Estelle Cuillerier

Book and Cover Design
Frédérique Bouvier

Book Layout
Marquis Interscript

Cover Photos
Getty Images © Monalyn Gracia
Shutterstock © TAVEESUK

Dedication

From my kindergarten teacher Miss Homa to my Ph.D. advisor
David Nunan, I thank the long line of teachers who taught me
to read, write, and think.

The publisher wishes to thank the following people for their helpful
comments and suggestions:
Joyce Akl, Algonquin College
Pamela Barkwell, Brock University
Devon Boucher, Thompson Rivers University
Kevin Countryman, Seneca College
Rachael Curtis, Alexander College
Jaime Demperio, Université du Québec à Montréal
Roisin Dewart, Université du Québec à Montréal
Tiffany MacDonald, East Coast School of Languages
Jason Toole, Wilfrid Laurier University
Hongfang Yu, Fanshawe College

INTRODUCTION

Welcome to *LEAP 1: Reading and Writing*. Language is the toolbox of the mind, letting you better understand the world and share your ideas about it. *LEAP* provides language skills necessary for success in college and university where you need to understand the details of new types of text, and take notes and ask questions in lectures. A cross-curricular approach gives you opportunities to explore new ideas from different academic disciplines including economics, engineering, and computer science. Within these disciplines are topics as diverse as innovation, business disruptions, DNA, and robotics. Along the way, the Pearson Global Scale of English (GSE) structures *LEAP 1's* learning goals as you build your high-frequency vocabulary with essential words from the Longman Communication 3000 and the Academic Word List.

LEAP 1: Reading and Writing helps you deal with challenging ideas. Different reading genres and perspectives from articles to infographics in each chapter help you work toward the reading and writing demands you encounter. Through carefully structured activities, you build your vocabulary and reading comprehension. Each chapter features focuses on reading, writing, critical thinking, grammar, and academic survival skills which support warm-up and final assignments. My eLab exercises and documents give you opportunities to reinforce and build on what you learn.

I am certain *LEAP 1: Reading and Writing* will be a key stepping-stone on your path to academic success.

ACKNOWLEDGEMENTS

The entire *LEAP* series is a grand collaboration fuelled by teachers who share time and ideas about student needs to help develop these print and online materials; my deepest thanks to all those teachers with whom I spoke at colleges, universities, and conferences. Thanks also to my gracious and supportive editors, Sharnee Chait and Linda Barton; their countless suggestions shaped this book. I'm grateful to the entire Pearson Canada team and Pearson teams in other countries I've had the privilege to visit including, this past year, Bulgaria, Colombia, Ecuador, Mexico, Peru, Poland, and the USA. And, as always, my thanks to Julia Williams, who pioneered the *LEAP* series.

Dr. Ken Beatty, Bowen Island, Canada

HIGHLIGHTS

Gearing Up uses images to spark critical thinking, reflection, and discussion about the chapter topic.

The **overview** outlines the chapter objectives.

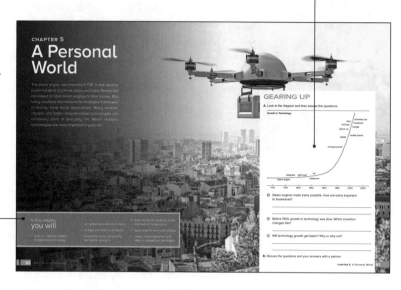

Vocabulary Build strengthens comprehension of key vocabulary words and reinforces them through tasks. Appendix 1 allows you to see how these words are rated in the Longman Communication 3000 and Academic Word List.

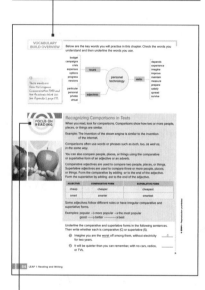

The three **readings** in each chapter offer a variety of perspectives on the chapter theme, providing content for writing tasks. The third reading is an authentic text from a magazine, a book, or an online news source. Key vocabulary words are in bold in the texts and difficult words are defined. Before, while, and after reading activities focus on comprehension and critical thinking.

Focus on Reading develops specific skills you need to fully understand content and structure of reading texts.

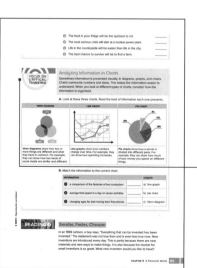

Focus on Critical Thinking introduces you to strategies for thinking critically about what you read and how to apply these strategies to writing tasks.

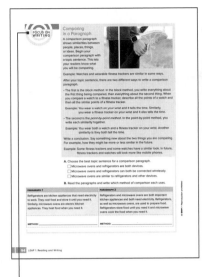

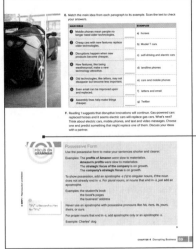

Focus on Grammar reviews important grammar features that you can apply in the writing assignments.

Focus on Writing develops key skills for writing effective English paragraphs.

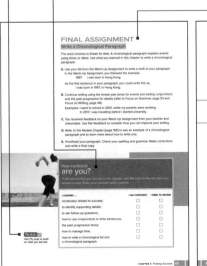

Academic Survival Skill helps you understand and practise effective classroom and study skills.

Warm-Up Assignment explores a writing task while preparing for the final assignment.

How confident are you? allows you to reflect on your learning and decide what you need to review. References to **My eLab** provide practice and additional content.

Final Assignment synthesizes the chapter content and theme through a writing task.

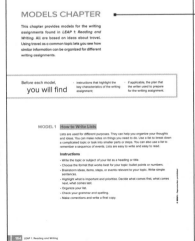

Models Chapter provides instructions and models for the writing tasks in the coursebook.

SCOPE AND SEQUENCE

CHAPTER	READING	CRITICAL THINKING	WRITING
CHAPTER 1 **THE LEARNING BRAIN** SUBJECT AREAS: education, technology	• Predicting before reading - Use title, subtitles, photos, and graphics to think about a topic	• Brainstorming using a mind map - Use a mind map to solve problems	• Reviewing simple sentences
CHAPTER 2 **NEW WAYS OF THINKING** SUBJECT AREAS: physics, sociology	• Finding the main idea in a text - Learn how to find the main idea in each paragraph	• Reflecting on what you read - Find meaning	• Writing compound sentences
CHAPTER 3 **FINDING SUCCESS** SUBJECT AREAS: business, economics	• Identifying supporting details - Find information that develops and supports main ideas	• Asking follow-up questions - Think of *wh-* questions while reading	• Using conjunctions to write sentences
CHAPTER 4 **DISRUPTING BUSINESS** SUBJECT AREAS: business, psychology	• Scanning for specific information - Look for key words	• Looking for examples - Find examples to support ideas	• Writing simple messages
CHAPTER 5 **A PERSONAL WORLD** SUBJECT AREAS: astronomy engineering	• Recognizing comparisons in a text - Use comparatives and superlatives to find comparisons	• Analyzing information in charts - Understand how information is organized in different charts	• Comparing in a paragraph
CHAPTER 6 **LIVING CODES** SUBJECT AREAS: genetics, geography	• Recognizing the main purpose of a text - Use the title and text organization to find the purpose	• Identifying facts and opinions - Understand the difference between opinions and valid opinions	• Writing an opinion paragraph
CHAPTER 7 **ROBOTS, AI, AND THE FUTURE** SUBJECT AREAS: computer science, medicine	• Recognizing a process in a text - Learn transition words	• Identifying problems and solutions - Identify topic sentences - Scan for key words	• Describing a process
CHAPTER 8 **LOOK INTO THE FUTURE** SUBJECT AREAS: communications, urban studies	• Making inferences when you read - Learn ways to reach a conclusion	• Using headings to understand ideas - Predict before you read	• Writing questions for a questionnaire

GRAMMAR	ACADEMIC SURVIVAL SKILL	ASSIGNMENTS	My eLab
• Modals: *can, could, should, have to*	• Checking and editing your writing - Identify common errors	• Writing a list of goals • Writing your goals in a paragraph	
• Simple past tense	• Remembering what you learn - Learn techniques to help you remember	• Describing an innovation • Writing a descriptive paragraph	

• Simple past and past progressive tenses	• Managing your time
	  - Plan an effective schedule
		• Writing a list of events
		• Writing a chronological paragraph
			• Online practice for each chapter:
			  - More comprehension exercises for the readings
			  - Vocabulary review
			  - Grammar practice
			  - Writing focus review
			  - Chapter test

• Possessive form	• Boosting your vocabulary
	  - Learn words that matter
		• Writing an informal message
		• Writing a formal email
			• Additional online reading texts:
			  - Extra readings with comprehension and critical thinking questions

• Future tense with *will* and *be going to*	• Working with others
	  - Learn tips for working in groups
		• Creating a Venn diagram
		• Writing a comparison paragraph
			• Study resources in Documents including:
			  - Irregular Verbs List

• Gerunds and infinitives	• Taking notes
	  - Remember what you read
		• Writing a table of facts and opinions
		• Writing an opinion paragraph
			- Proofreading and Editing Tips
			  - Writing Assignment Checklist

• Prepositions of time: *at, in, on*	• Studying smarter - Find ways to be efficient and effective	• Writing steps in a process • Writing a process paragraph	
• Present perfect tense	• Preparing for exams - Learn strategies to help you succeed	• Writing a short questionnaire • Writing about your findings	

TABLE OF CONTENTS

The Learning Brain

Humans are weak and slow compared to many other animals. But our human brains set us apart. We are successful because we can think and plan, use complex tools, and adapt to new situations. Some people wonder if we are now creating computers and robots that will someday replace us. This is unlikely as long as we continue to learn and to look for new ways to solve problems. How do you learn?

In this chapter, you will

- learn vocabulary related to learning;
- predict before reading;
- brainstorm using a mind map;
- review simple sentences;
- review modals;
- learn how to check and edit your writing;
- write a list of goals and then write it as a paragraph.

GEARING UP

A. Look at the illustration and then answer the questions.

Left and Right Sides of the Brain

logical
plans
looks for details

creative
flexible
looks for general ideas

1 Name something new you would like to learn.

_____

2 Which side of your brain would be the most helpful in learning it?

_____

3 Name something you learn with the other side of your brain.

_____

4 Name something you learn using both sides of your brain.

_____

B. Discuss the questions and your answers with a partner.

Below are the key words you will practise in this chapter. Check the words you understand and then underline the words you use.

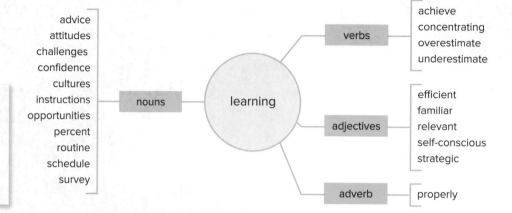

advice
attitudes
challenges
confidence
cultures
instructions
opportunities
percent
routine
schedule
survey

nouns — learning

verbs
achieve
concentrating
overestimate
underestimate

adjectives
efficient
familiar
relevant
self-conscious
strategic

adverb
properly

These words are from the Longman Communication 3000 and the Academic Word List. See Appendix 1, page 172.

FOCUS ON READING

Predicting Before Reading

To predict something means to guess at what might happen. Before you read, look at the different parts of the text. Do the following to help you predict what a text might be about.

• Read the title.

• Read the subtitles.

• Look at the photos.

• Review other graphics, such as diagrams, charts, and tables.

Taking clues from these parts of a text will help you think about the topic. When you read, you can check whether or not your predictions were right. If your predictions were wrong, ask yourself what you may have missed from the clues.

A. Here are the titles of the three readings in this chapter. Choose the answer that best predicts what the reading will be about.

1 Reading 1, "Never Too Late to Learn" is about _____.

   a) how to be on time more often

   b) what to do when you're late

   c) how you can learn at any age

2 Reading 2, "Ten Tips and Tricks to Learn Any Language" is about _____.

   a) the best ways to learn a language

   b) the fastest ways to learn a language

   c) who is able to learn a language

3 Reading 3, "How Do You Study?" is about _____.

   a) missing your exams

   b) a variety of study tips

   c) not studying for exams

B. Visual clues help you make predictions. Look at the photo at the beginning of Reading 1 (page 8). Now that you have more information, does it change your mind about your choice?

The photo suggests the reading is about _____

_____

Brainstorming Using a Mind Map

When you brainstorm, especially in a group, you think of new ideas and other ways to solve problems. A mind map works in much the same way: you start with one idea and connect it to other ideas. A mind map is useful for brainstorming ideas.

A. When you think of a new idea, don't stop to consider whether it is a good one or not—you can do that later. Write three ideas you think about when you read the term *language learning*.

• _____

• _____

• _____

B. Draw three more bubbles with other ideas about language learning on this mind map. Start from the centre bubble or from one of the other bubbles. For example, next to *Internet*, you might add *language games*.

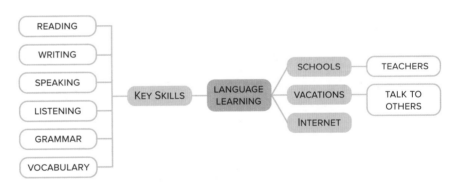

C. Mind maps show how ideas relate to each other. Cross out the word that does not belong in each line.

❶ teachers, students, books, tutors, professors

❷ colleges, online classes, universities, technical schools, computers

❸ charts, diagrams, magazines, illustrations, graphs

 **Never Too Late to Learn**

Learning new things can be difficult. Some things, like learning to ride a bicycle, can take weeks. Other things, like learning a second language, can take years. The key is motivation: having reasons to learn something new.

VOCABULARY BUILD

In the following exercises, explore key words from Reading 1.

A. The word *challenge* can be used as a noun or as a verb. As a noun, it means *something difficult*. As a verb, it means *invite someone to try*. Indicate whether each word in the table is a noun or a verb, or both.

WORDS	NOUN	VERB	BOTH
❶ achieve			
❷ cultures			
❸ instructions			
❹ opportunities			
❺ percent			
❻ survey			

B. Match each word to its definition.

WORDS		DEFINITIONS
❶ achieve	_____	a) groups with their own customs
❷ cultures	_____	b) chances for success
❸ instructions	_____	c) part of 100
❹ opportunities	_____	d) steps on how to do something
❺ percent	_____	e) reach a result or objective by skill

C. What do the words in bold mean to you? Complete the sentences.

❶ What is something you want to **achieve**?

I want to achieve _____

❷ What is one **challenge** you face when learning English?

One challenge is _____

❸ Which is your favourite **culture**?

My favourite culture is _____

❹ When do you need **instructions**?

I need instructions _____

❺ What is a fun **opportunity** you have?

A fun opportunity is _____

Before You Read

A. Reading 1 mentions reasons students learn a second language. What are your reasons? Brainstorm four reasons and write them in the mind map.

WHY LEARN A LANGUAGE

B. Predict one reason you think might be discussed in Reading 1.

_____

C. Look at the bar chart. It is the results of a survey that show what some British students think are the benefits to learning a second language. Indicate whether or not you agree with the results of the survey. Then discuss with a partner.

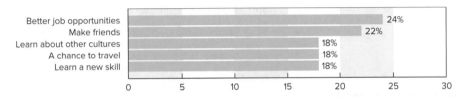

LEARNING A SECOND LANGUAGE CAN HELP ME ...	AGREE	DON'T AGREE
1 get a better job.		
2 make friends.		
3 learn about other cultures.		
4 get a chance to travel.		
5 learn a new skill.		

While You Read

D. In Focus on Reading (page 4) you made predictions about this reading based on the title and the photo. While you read, check if your predictions were correct.

translate (v.): express words in another language

greater powers (n.): more abilities

determined (adj.): planned with a firm decision

experts (n.): people who know a lot about a topic

participated (v.): involved or took part in

amateur (adj.): not professional

Why learn a second language? On a **survey**, 1,001 British teenagers have different reasons. Twenty-four **percent** think a second language could
5 improve their job **opportunities**. Many students get jobs in the service industry, such as working in stores, restaurants, and banks. It's helpful to speak more than one language. Speaking more than one language may also mean they get paid more.

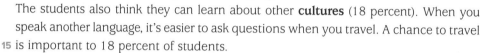

10 Many students (22 percent) think a second language can help them make friends. This is because they can talk to people who don't speak their language. The students also think they can learn about other **cultures** (18 percent). When you speak another language, it's easier to ask questions when you travel. A chance to travel
15 is important to 18 percent of students.

A final reason (18 percent) is to learn a new skill. There are probably several parts to this point. A second language can help you:

- find out about skills used by other language speakers, such as how to cook;

- learn in a place where your first language isn't used;

20 - **translate instructions** into another language.

But there are other reasons for learning things. When teacher and writer John Holt was forty years old, he wanted to learn something new: how to play the cello. He wrote about it in a book called *Never Too Late*. The book explains the steps Holt took to learn the cello. He wrote about the people he met, and his many **challenges**. Holt said,

25   If I could learn to play the cello well, as I thought I could, I could show
        by my own example that we all have **greater powers** than we think;
        that whatever we want to learn or learn to do, we probably can learn;
        that our lives and our possibilities are not **determined** and fixed by
        what happened to us when we were little, or by what **experts** say we
30   can or cannot do. (p. 185)

What Holt means is that many people do not try something new, like learning a language, because they think they are too old. Sometimes they don't try because experts say it's too difficult.

Holt practised the cello three to four hours a day. He took lessons, read music
35 magazines, went to concerts, and played music with friends. He **participated** in two **amateur** orchestras. He listened to music played by great cello players. After a year, a friend asked, "Would you teach my young son?"

Holt was surprised. "I'm barely a beginner!" he said. But he started to teach the student. Teaching also helped Holt improve.

40 The students in the survey felt good when they learned another language. This is the best reason to learn a second language or to learn anything else: to challenge yourself and **achieve** something new.

(459 words)

Reference

Holt, J. (1991). *Never too late: My musical life story.* New York: Addison-Wesley.

> **Vocabulary Tip:**
> Read words in context. Guess the meaning of a word from the words around it.

After You Read

E. Indicate whether these statements are true or false, according to the text.

STATEMENTS		TRUE	FALSE
1	Many students think a second language could improve their job opportunities.		
2	Learning about other cultures is not important to the students.		
3	One practical skill was to be able to translate instructions.		
4	John Holt learned to play the cello because experts said he could.		
5	To learn the cello, Holt tried many different things, such as playing music with friends.		
6	Holt was not surprised to be asked to teach a young student.		

F. Choose the word or phrase in parentheses that best completes each sentence.

1 Students think about travelling to countries where English (is / <u>is not</u>) spoken.

2 Translating instructions might be useful for (medical / grammar) problems.

3 A beginner (cannot / can) teach others.

4 Learning a second language or learning the cello are both (easy / difficult).

5 Learning something new helps you to (achieve / lose) something.

FOCUS ON WRITING

Reviewing Simple Sentences

A sentence begins with a capital letter and ends with a punctuation mark—a period (.), a question mark (?), or an exclamation mark (!). Most sentences are short, and not complex. A simple sentence only needs a subject and a verb to be a complete thought.

Examples: Holt was surprised.
subject ⌐ ⌐ verb

A final point on the survey is a sense of achievement.
↑ ↑
subject verb

Students chose three main reasons.
↑ ↑
subject verb

This example has a compound subject and a compound verb but it's still a simple sentence.

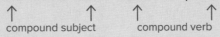
Holt and his student studied and practised.
↑ ↑ ↑ ↑
compound subject compound verb

A simple sentence is called *an independent clause* because it stands on its own.

▶

© **ERPI** • Reproduction prohibited

CHAPTER 1 The Learning Brain **9**

A. Unscramble these words to write simple sentences. Remember to capitalize the first word of each sentence.

① language / how / you / do / your / learn / first /?

How do you [learn] *your first language?*

② hear / practise / you / you / what /.

_____

③ create / in / head / rules / your / you /.

_____

④ make / you / and / frequent / mistakes / common /.

_____

⑤ learn / you / mistakes / your / from /.

_____

⑥ help / mistakes / improve / to / you /.

_____

B. Read your sentences again. Highlight the subject and circle the verb in each one.

C. Write three simple sentences about *learning*. Check your sentences with a partner.

① _____

② _____

③ _____

READING 2

Ten Tips and Tricks to Learn Any Language

Some people speak many languages. Reading 2 is based on an interview with Matthew Youlden. He speaks nine languages and understands many others. His brother Michael speaks many languages too. Read Mathew's tips for learning a new language.

VOCABULARY BUILD

In the following exercises, explore key words from Reading 2.

A. Fill in the blanks with the correct words to complete the sentences.

advice	confidence	properly	self-conscious
attitudes	familiar	~~relevant~~	

① I wasn't aware of the _____*relevant*_____ rule about late assignments.

② The best _____ is to treat others the way you want to be treated.

3. People can be _____ about the opinions of others.

4. People's _____ toward language learning are often old.

5. If you don't have _____, you may not want to try new things.

6. To study _____, most people need a quiet place.

7. Are you _____ with the other students in your class?

B. The word *properly* is an adverb. Adverbs describe verbs. You can change adjectives into adverbs by adding *-ly*. Write each adjective as an adverb.

1. confident ___*confidently*___

2. familiar _____

3. relevant _____

4. self-conscious _____

C. What do the words in bold mean to you? Complete the sentences.

1. What **advice** can you give another student?

   My advice is _____

2. What do you have **confidence** doing?

   I have confidence _____

3. Which subjects in college are you **familiar** with?

   I'm familiar with _____

4. When do you have to write **properly**?

   I have to write properly _____

5. What course in college is **relevant** to your future job?

   The relevant course is _____

Before You Read

A. Look at the photo and predict how it might relate to Reading 2. Complete the sentences.

1. The woman looks _____

2. The photo shows _____

3. Reading 2 is about _____

   _____

B. What are good ways to learn new words? Look at the mind map and brainstorm two other ideas. Discuss with a partner.

```
                              ┌──────────────────────────┐
                              │  WRITE WORDS ON CARDS    │
                              │    AND REVIEW THEM        │
                              └──────────────────────────┘
  ┌──────────────────┐                ┌──────────────────────────┐
  │ LOOK UP WORDS    │                │                          │
  │ IN A DICTIONARY  │──┐             │                          │
  └──────────────────┘  │  ┌────────────────┐                   │
                        └──│ LEARN NEW WORDS │──┐                │
  ┌──────────────────┐  ┌──└────────────────┘  └──────────────────────────┘
  │ LEARN NEW WORDS  │──┘
  │ THAT YOU READ    │                ┌──────────────────────────┐
  └──────────────────┘                │                          │
                                      │                          │
                                      └──────────────────────────┘
```

While You Read

C. While you read, underline the tips. Read a second time and circle the tips that are most useful to you.

Ten Tips and Tricks to Learn Any Language

fluently (adv.): quickly and easily

motivated (adj.): encouraged to do something

myth (n.): old story

comfort zone (n.): in control, comfortable

constantly (adv.): all the time

imitate (v.): copy someone else

Matthew Youlden can speak nine languages **fluently**. But he can understand a dozen or so more. How could you learn to speak another language? These ten tips are Youlden's **advice**.

5 1. Know why you learn.
You need a good reason to learn another language. In fact, you should think of many reasons to learn a new language.

2. Find a partner.
Matthew learned several languages 10 with his brother Michael. They started with Greek at age eight. They were very **motivated**. You should have someone to speak to. Your partner can help you keep learning.

15 3. Talk to yourself.
When you can't speak to anyone else, talk to yourself. You should practise to remember new words and phrases. This can build your **confidence**.

20 4. Keep it **relevant**.
Talking to people can help make learning relevant for you. You have to use a new language to learn it. Use it in everyday settings.

5. Have fun.
Be creative with your new language. Think of fun ways to practise. You could write a 25 poem or simply talk to strangers.

6. Act like a child.
The idea that children are better learners than adults is a **myth**. But learn the **attitudes** of children. Don't be **self-conscious**. Play in the language and be willing to make mistakes. You can learn though mistakes.

30 7. Leave your **comfort zone**.
Don't be afraid to try new things. You can talk to strangers, ask for directions, order food, or try to tell a joke.

8. Listen.
Learn to listen before you speak. Every language can sound strange the first time you 35 hear it. The more you hear it, the more **familiar** it becomes, and the easier it is to speak it **properly**. The best way to learn could be to hear new sounds **constantly**.

9. Watch people talk.
Different languages need you to use your tongue, lips, and throat in different ways. Pronunciation uses both your body and your brain. Look at people saying new words 40 and sounds. Watch them in person or on video. Then you should try to **imitate** their sounds.

dive in (v.): get completely involved in something

10. **Dive in.**

Is there a best way to learn? You should practise your new language every single day. You will want to remember as much as possible right from the start. So if you learn
45 something, try to use it all day. As the week progresses, try to think in the new language, try to write in it, and try to speak it to yourself.

(409 words)

Reference

Jordan, J-E. (2016). Ten tips and tricks to learn any language. *Babbel Magazine*. Retrieved from https://www.babbel.com/en/magazine/10-tips-from-an-expert

After You Read

D. Choose the phrase that best completes each sentence, according to the text.

➊ People who have a good reason to learn another language are _____.
   a) less likely to be motivated
   b) likely to ignore motivations
   c) more likely to be motivated

➋ Matthew and Michael are brothers who _____.
   a) don't speak the same languages
   b) studied languages together
   c) only speak Greek together

➌ Speaking to yourself is one way
   of _____.
   a) not having to listen to others
   b) practising when you are alone
   c) asking questions

➍ Writing a poem in a new language
   is _____.
   a) a fun way to practise
   b) required for university
   c) a common test strategy

➎ It's a myth that children learn languages _____.
   a) more easily than adults
   b) less easily than adults
   c) as frequently as adults

➏ Listening to a new language makes it _____.
   a) more difficult to speak properly
   b) difficult to speak your own language
   c) easier to speak it properly

E. Read tips 9 and 10 again. Choose the best summary of the two tips.

☐ Imitate sounds you know by ignoring people's facial expressions and practise when with others.

☐ Learn new sounds by imitating people's facial expressions and practise as much as you can.

☐ Imitate new sounds in your first language by practising new facial expressions once a week.

F. Check the reasons why you might *not* follow some of the tips.

☐ You are too shy to talk to other people.

☐ You don't have the time.

☐ You might not know anyone to talk to.

☐ People may not want to talk to you.

☐ You don't need to learn another language.

FOCUS ON GRAMMAR

Modals: *Can, Could, Should, Have to*

Reading 2 has many examples of *can, could, should,* and *have to*. These words are *modals*. A modal is an auxiliary verb used with a main verb. Modals add meaning to sentences.

MODALS	MEANINGS	EXAMPLES
can	permission: you have a choice	You **can** use my dictionary while you study.
	ability: you are able to do something	You **can** get better grades if you study.
could	possibility: you do something if you want to	You **could** study this afternoon.
should	suggestion or advice: you make the right choice for you	You **should** study for your test.
have to	obligation: you have no choice	You **have to** study to pass your exam.

A. Choose the modal in parentheses that correctly completes each sentence.

1 Matthew Youlden (can / could) speak nine languages.

2 You (could / should) listen to podcasts to improve a new language.

3 You (can / should) have someone to speak to.

4 Talking to people (can / have to) keep the learning process relevant for you.

5 You (have to / can) use a language to learn it.

6 I (could / have to) practise English with a partner.

7 When I finish my homework, (can / should) I watch a movie?

8 I only have one hour so I (should / have to) study for the English test.

9 You (should / have to) look up a new word in the dictionary.

10 I know I (can / have to) finish my English homework in twenty minutes.

B. Draw an arrow ↓ to indicate where the modal in parentheses should be placed in each sentence.

1 (can) I↓see the library is closed after school today .

2 (have to) It doesn't matter because I finish my homework tonight .

3 (could) We do our homework tomorrow if you want .

4 (can) Lisa, we agree on a time to meet ?

5 (should) It be some time before dinner .

6 (can) We do our homework at the downtown library, if you like .

My eLab ✎

Visit My eLab to complete Grammar Review exercises for this chapter.

WARM-UP ASSIGNMENT
Write a List of Goals

Goals are things you want to do. Language learning goals can help you improve your English or another language.

A. Write a list of your language learning goals. Refer to the Models Chapter (page 164) to see an example of a list and to learn more about how to write one.

B. Use what you learned about writing sentences in Focus on Writing (page 9), and what you learned about modals in Focus on Grammar (page 14). Write four goals that could help you improve your English.

Example: I should improve my English grammar.

1 I can _____

2 I could _____

3 I should _____

4 I have to _____

C. Check your list. Are all the words spelled correctly? Is your grammar correct?

D. Read your list aloud. Are there any other errors? Make corrections and write your final copy.

E. Share your list with a partner.

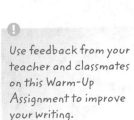

Use feedback from your teacher and classmates on this Warm-Up Assignment to improve your writing.

How Do You Study?

You take many exams. What's the best way to study for an exam? Do you like to study on your own, or with friends? Do you like to study at home, at school, or at the library? Reading 3 suggests you should sometimes take a day off. Why might that be a good way to help prepare for an exam?

VOCABULARY BUILD

In the following exercises, explore key words from Reading 3.

A. Many words are made up of smaller words, such as *over* in *overestimate* and *under* in *underestimate*. Understanding parts of a word can make it easier to understand the whole word. Write the word that matches each definition. If you cannot guess, look up the words *overestimate* and *underestimate* in a dictionary.

_____: think something is smaller or less important than it is

_____: think something is larger or more important than it is

B. Choose the phrase that best completes each sentence. Key words are in bold.

① When I put studying on my **schedule**, I _____.
   a) know when I will do it
   b) can do it any time I want

② **Concentrating** on just one subject

   means you _____.
   a) will do better in all your subjects
   b) may forget about some subjects

③ A **strategic** way to learn

   is _____.
   a) to forget about having any plans
   b) to study the most important things first

④ It's most **efficient** _____.
   a) to leave your studying to the day before a test
   b) to study several times before the day of a test

⑤ Part of my study **routine** includes

   _____.
   a) talking about questions with friends
   b) playing video games with friends

⑥ I usually overestimate _____.
   a) the time I have to study
   b) how little time I have

C. What do the words in bold mean to you? Complete the sentences.

① What is something you're **concentrating** on?

I'm concentrating on _____

② When are you most **efficient**?

I'm most efficient _____

③ What is something you **overestimate**?

I overestimate _____

④ What is the most important part of your daily **routine**?

The most important part is _____

⑤ What do you always put on your **schedule**?

I always put _____ on my schedule.

My eLab

Visit My eLab to complete Vocabulary Review exercises for this chapter.

Before You Read

A. Think about when you study for an exam. What are things you *should* do, *could* do, *have to* do, and *can* do? Brainstorm to fill in the mind map.

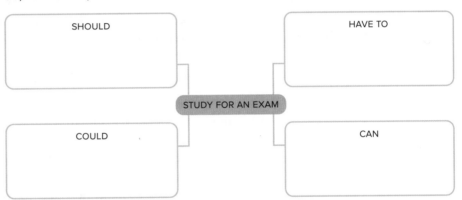

B. Read these tips from Reading 3. For each one, choose the answer that best predicts what the rest of the tip will be about.

① What's worse than being stressed is being around stressed people.

   a) Stressed people can help your chances to study.

   b) Stressed people can hurt your chances to study.

   c) Stressed people usually study harder than others.

② Don't underestimate your efficiency (how well you work).

   a) It's likely that you are not organized.

   b) Estimating things is a waste of time.

   c) You are probably quite organized.

③ Stick to the 80/20 rule.

   a) Spend 80 percent of your time on 20 percent of the most important things.

   b) Spend 100 percent of your time on 100 percent of the most important things.

   c) Spend 20 percent of your time on 80 percent of the most important things.

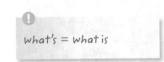

what's = what is

④ Don't change your routines too much (even your social plans).

    a) Your social plans should include studying.

    b) It's important to relax and not study all the time.

    c) If you have a study routine, don't have social plans.

⑤ What's worse than not studying is pretending to study.

    a) Study even if you are too tired.

    b) You won't be tired if you study hard.

    c) Don't try to study if you are too tired.

While You Read

C. While you read, compare your notes from Before You Read, task A, with the ideas in the text. Underline the things that could help you study.

How Do You Study?

false reality (n.): idea that is not true

ground-breaking (n.): something new and impressive

mental framework (n.): way of thinking about things

Here are a few tips for university students during exam season.

1. What's worse than being stressed is being around stressed people.
Don't surround yourself with people who constantly remind you of all the work you
5 haven't done. This is essentially going to create a **false reality** for you—feeling as though you are more behind than you actually are. You end up so concerned with how much work you have, that you don't spend time **concentrating** on *how* and *where* to start studying.

2. Don't underestimate your efficiency.
10 Just as it's important not to **overestimate** your ability to study a certain amount of content in a given time, it's equally important to also not **underestimate** yourself. What you may think takes a week to study, may only really be a day's worth of *efficient* work. The key word here is *efficient*. This is no **ground-breaking** idea; the key is developing a **mental framework** to judge your own abilities.

rational (adj.): reasonable

merits (n.): good points

overhaul (v.): redo completely

accommodate (v.): make room for

15 3. Stick to the 80/20 rule.

Be **rational**, focus 80 percent of your effort on the top 20 percent important concepts, themes, or ideas of your exam content. Only spend 20 percent of your effort on the 80 percent less-important things. Taking an exam is equally **strategic** as it is about the **merits** of your knowledge.

20 4. Don't change your routines too much (even your social plans).

The last thing you want to do is to change your daily **routine**. If you usually hang out with friends on weekends, don't let exams turn you into a hermit crab. It's easy to panic—changing your **schedule** is one way to do this.

There are instances where you have no choice but to **overhaul** your schedule to 25 **accommodate** studying. That's when post-secondary education fails students. But don't give up sleep and social routines.

5. What's worse than not studying is pretending to study.

The amount of time you put into studying is not important. Pretending to study is worse than knowing that you don't know. Don't study if you know that it's just one 30 of those days where your mind is wandering. It's the smarter way.

It's normal not to be able to study sometimes. Take a day off if you have to because then you will be aware of how much you don't know, and also be refreshed.

(387 words)

Houshmand, K. (2014, December 12). How to study for an exam? Take a day off. *Globe and Mail*. Retrieved from http://www.theglobeandmail.com/news/national/education/how-to-study-for-an-exam-take-a-day-off/article22052326/

After You Read

D. Indicate which of the following you *should do* and which you *should not do*, according to the text.

STATEMENTS	SHOULD DO	SHOULD NOT DO
❶ Be with people who remind you of the work you haven't done.		
❷ Concentrate on *how* and *where* to start studying.		
❸ Learn to judge your own abilities.		
❹ Spend 80 percent of the time focused on 20 percent of the most important concepts.		
❺ Change your daily routine.		
❻ Give up sleep to study more.		
❼ Force yourself to study even if you are having trouble concentrating.		
❽ Take a day off.		

E. Check your predictions from Before You Read, task B. Which are correct? Which would you change? Discuss with a partner.

Checking and Editing Your Writing

English grammar has many rules. For example, you must start a sentence with a capital letter and end it with a punctuation mark. When you check your work, follow these rules and other spelling and grammar rules. Here are some ways you can check your work.

• Take a break! It's not easy to check your work right after you write it. Wait a half hour or more and then look at it again. You may see errors.

• Read your work aloud. Sometimes you will hear mistakes.

• Use a computer spell checker, but make sure the dictionary is set to your form of English. American or British English are common, but your country may use a different form.

• Use a computer grammar checker. But check the suggestions. They are not always perfect!

A. Circle the error in each sentence and then make the correction.

CORRECTION

❶ Computers save a lot of time? _____

❷ Rather than go to school, studnts
can take classes from home. _____

❸ there are tutors to help students. _____

❹ Suchstudents can work early mornings
and late evenings. _____

❺ Student can exchange information. _____

❻ He can help each other solve problems. _____

B. Edit this paragraph. There are four errors. Cross out each error and write the correction above it.

> *In*
> ~~in~~ 1929, Margaret Dunning decided to go to university to study business.
>
> But the economy wes bad. Instead, Margaret went to work at her mother's
>
> bank? In 1949, she bought a car and kept it in good condition When she
>
> turned 102, a company that sells car parts paid her tuition at the University
>
> of Michigan so she could completea degree.

C. Now that you know more about editing, look again at your Warm-Up Assignment. Are there any errors you missed?

> Remember to also look for extra spaces.

> The computer might fix some errors. Look at the corrections and learn from your mistakes.

FINAL ASSIGNMENT

Write Your Goals in a Paragraph

Use what you learned in this chapter to write your list of language learning goals in a paragraph.

A. Use your list from the Warm-Up Assignment to write a draft of your paragraph.

B. You received feedback on your Warm-Up Assignment from your teacher and classmates. Use this feedback to consider how you can improve your writing.

C. Build on what you learned in Focus on Writing (page 9). Begin with a simple sentence that introduces your goals.

Example: I have four language learning goals.

D. After you write your four goals, end with a sentence that concludes your ideas with something you *can* do, *could* do, *should* do, or *have to* do.

Example: I **can** start working on my goals today.

E. Refer to the Models Chapter (page 165) to see an example of a paragraph and to learn more about how to write one.

F. Proofread your paragraph. Check your spelling, grammar, and punctuation.

G. Read your paragraph aloud. Are there any other errors? Make corrections and write a final copy.

How confident
are you?

Think about what you learned in this chapter. Use the table to decide what you should review. Share your answers with a partner.

I LEARNED ...	I AM CONFIDENT	I NEED TO REVIEW
vocabulary related to learning;	☐	☐
to predict before reading;	☐	☐
to brainstorm using a mind map;	☐	☐
about simple sentences;	☐	☐
how to use modals;	☐	☐
how to check and edit my writing;	☐	☐
how to write a list of goals and then write it as a paragraph.	☐	☐

My eLab 🖊

Visit My eLab to build on what you learned.

CHAPTER 2

New Ways of Thinking

Have you ever put a shoe on the wrong foot? Until 1800, left and right shoes did not exist. Before then, shoes usually fit either foot. Making the first shoes was a major innovation—a new invention that improved life. Making shoes for left and right feet was a minor innovation. Major and minor innovations come from critical and creative thinking when people look at old problems in new ways.

In this chapter, you will

- learn vocabulary related to innovation;

- find the main idea in a text;
- reflect on what you read;
- review the simple past tense;
- write compound sentences;

- discover ways to remember what you learn;
- write a description of an innovation and a descriptive paragraph.

GEARING UP

A. A SWOT diagram can help you understand how you and your ideas can succeed. Look at this SWOT analysis diagram. Imagine you wanted to start a ride-sharing app. Then answer the questions.

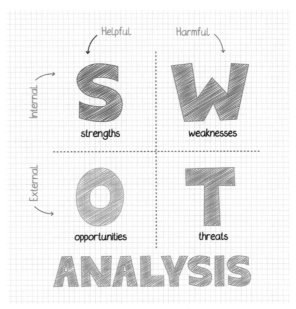

① What is one of your strengths? For example, do you know how to drive a car or write computer code?

_____

② What is a weakness you have? For example, which skills from other people would help make your app successful?

_____

③ What is an opportunity offered by your app? For example, why would people use it?

_____

④ What is a threat to your app? For example, is someone already doing something similar?

_____

B. Discuss the questions and your answers with a partner.

Below are the key words you will practise in this chapter. Check the words you understand. and then underline the words you use.

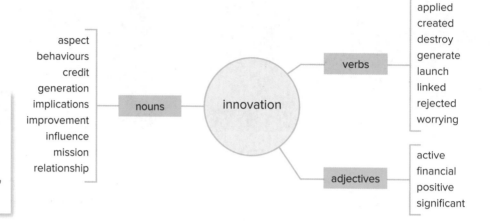

nouns

innovation

verbs

adjectives

aspect
behaviours
credit
generation
implications
improvement
influence
mission
relationship

applied
created
destroy
generate
launch
linked
rejected
worrying

active
financial
positive
significant

These words are from the Longman Communication 3000 and the Academic Word List. See Appendix 1, page 172.

FOCUS ON READING

Finding the Main Idea in a Text

When someone asks you about a movie or a novel, you answer briefly—in a sentence or two—rather than telling the whole story. Your answer is usually the *main idea*. When you read a paragraph, the main idea is often the first or second sentence. But a writer can put the main idea later in the paragraph as well. Here are some ways you can find the main idea in a text.

• Read the paragraph. Ask yourself what it is about.

• Look for words or ideas that are repeated; these might indicate the main idea.

• Ignore questions and examples; these are seldom main ideas.

Sometimes the main idea of the first paragraph is the main idea of the whole reading.

A. Read this excerpt from Reading 1. Underline the main idea. Discuss with a partner.

> Writer Scott Berkun (2013) dislikes the word *innovation* for a few reasons. He defines innovation as "a significant positive change" (para. 3) but he thinks that the term is overused. He argues that individuals and organizations give themselves the label without really thinking what it means. Nor do they have evidence to show what they do is really innovative.

Leonardo da Vinci
(1452–1519)

da Vinci's flying machine

B. Read these pairs of sentences and choose the sentence that is a main idea.

1 a) For example, at that time, there was a new electric chair.

   b) Edison suggested alternating current was dangerous.

2 a) The story explains different sides of innovation.

   b) Sometimes it's just an idea and sometimes it's hard work.

3 a) Innovation is about new ways of thinking and doing things.

   b) Were Marie Curie and Leonardo da Vinci both innovators?

FOCUS ON CRITICAL THINKING

Reflecting on What You Read

Reflecting is an important critical thinking skill. When you read and reflect, you ask yourself what the text means to you and how it compares to your ideas and experience. Once you know the main idea, follow these suggestions.

• Ask yourself how it relates to what you already know.

• Look at the examples. Do they support the main idea?

• Do you agree with what is written? Why or why not?

• Consider what you need to learn more about.

Thomas Edison
(1847–1931)

A. Read this excerpt about Nikola Tesla, from Reading 2. Underline the ideas that you already know. For example, do you know about New York City, Nikola Tesla, Thomas Edison, or the difference between AC and DC?

> After moving to New York City, Tesla went to work for one of the greatest inventors in history, Thomas Edison. The relationship did not last long, and Tesla left to invent on his own. Tesla's greatest invention was the idea of alternating current (AC), which is now used in most electric devices from light bulbs to washing machines. It was the opposite of Edison's version of direct current (DC), used in batteries. Edison did everything he could to destroy interest in Tesla's innovation. For example, at that time a new electric chair was introduced for executions. It used alternating current and Edison shared that fact to suggest alternating current was dangerous.

B. Now highlight ideas you need to learn more about.

READING 1   Significant Positive Change

American politician Robert Kennedy (1925–1968) said, "There are those who look at things the way they are, and ask why? I dream of things that never were, and ask why not?" This is the spirit of innovation. Innovation is about new ways of thinking and doing things. The invention of the video camera was based on the work of earlier inventors but it was still a major innovation. Since then, others have introduced minor innovations, including adding video cameras to mobile phones.

In the following exercises, explore key words from Reading 1.

A. Fill in the blanks with the correct words to complete the paragraph.

aspect	behaviours	improvement	significant

One _____ difference between the _____

of innovators and other people is that innovators seldom take time off. Finding

solutions to problems through innovation is exciting and innovators want to do

it all the time. Once they discover a key _____ of one problem

and find an _____, they want to start on the next problem.

B. Write definitions for these words. If you need help, use a dictionary.

1. applied (v.): *used on something* _____

2. positive (adj.): _____

3. significant (adj.): _____

4. worrying (v.): _____

C. What do the words in bold mean to you? Complete the sentences.

1. Which one **aspect** of school do you like most?

   I like _____

2. What is a **behaviour** you like in other people?

   I like _____

3. What is a personal **improvement** you would like to make?

   I'd like to _____

   _____

4. What is something you feel **positive** about?

   I feel positive about _____

   _____

5. What's the most **significant** thing you've done this year?

   I have _____

   _____

Before You Read

A. Consider the title of Reading 1, "Significant Positive Change." How do you think
it relates to the theme of innovation? Choose the best answer.

☐ It explains that some innovations are bad.

☐ It is a short definition of innovation.

☐ It is a challenge to improve innovations.

B. Reading 1 is about improving a product—a video camera—in an innovative way. Innovations also improve services. Read the examples and write one more for each type of innovation.

➊ innovative products: *mobile phones,* _____

_____

➋ innovative services: *music downloads,* _____

_____

While You Read

C. While you read, underline the main idea in each paragraph.

Significant Positive Change

solve (v.): find an answer to a problem

confused (adj.): uncertain about something

get rid of (v.): take away

memorable (adj.): worth remembering or easily remembered

Writer Scott Berkun (2013) dislikes the word *innovation* for a few reasons. He defines innovation as "a significant positive change" (para. 3) but he thinks that the term is overused. He argues that individuals and organizations give themselves the label
5 without really thinking what it means. Nor do they have evidence to show what they do is really innovative.

It may be difficult to measure what *significant* means, but *positive change* is clearer. Positive change means an **improvement** of some kind. Innovation is often used to refer to technology. But the definition is broader than that. An innovation can be
10 improvements in anything. For example, a good advertisement can change people's bad **behaviours**.

A large part of innovation is critical and creative thinking. Many innovators look at a problem and wonder how to **solve** it in a new way. One example is the story of a meeting between the chief engineer at a Japanese electronics company and the
15 company's top designer. The engineer asked the designer to bring the company's latest video camera and a bucket of water to her office. The designer was **confused**, but followed the instructions. "Imagine if I put the new video camera into the bucket of water," the engineer said. "What would happen?"

The designer didn't quite understand, but offered a few answers. Finally, when he was
20 saying that small bubbles of air would disappear, the engineer smiled. "That's right. Now go back to work and **get rid of** all that air." The engineer meant that she wanted the designer to lose all of the extra space in the video camera to make it smaller.

Who was the innovator—the engineer or the designer? In fact, they both were innovating,
25 in different ways. The designer was working hard to make a good video camera but wasn't **worrying** about how it could be smaller. The engineer was thinking about how it could be made smaller but was looking for a way to
30 explain that to the designer in a **memorable** way. By thinking about making the video camera smaller, the engineer was innovating. So was the designer, who found ways to make improvements.

!
This extended example makes the ideas easier to follow and remember. When you read, think of your own examples.

analyzing (v.): examining in a careful way to explain something

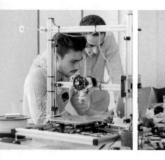

35 The story explains different **aspects** of innovation. Sometimes it is just an idea and sometimes it's hard work. Sometimes one person takes on various jobs, seeing problems, thinking of solutions, and developing them. Sometimes these duties are spread among a team, working together to make something new. Innovation comes from trying to understand everyday things, asking questions, experimenting with new 40 ideas, and **analyzing** the results. These are general skills that can be **applied** to every challenge you encounter.

(429 words)

Reference

Berkun, S. (2013, April 3). The best definition of innovation. Scott Berkun. Retrieved from http://scottberkun.com/2013/the-best-definition-of-innovation/

After You Read

D. For each paragraph, choose the main idea that is closest to what you underlined in the reading.

PARAGRAPH 1:

a) Innovation can be defined as a significant positive change.

b) It is important to be able to give a definition of innovation.

PARAGRAPH 2:

a) Innovators use expert skills to change the world.

b) Innovations can be improvements in anything.

PARAGRAPH 3:

a) Innovators wonder how to solve unknown problems.

b) Critical and creative thinking help solve problems.

PARAGRAPH 4:

a) The designer realized the correct answer.

b) The engineer learned about air bubbles.

PARAGRAPH 5:

a) Air bubbles are a problem in underwater video cameras.

b) People have different roles in finding ways to innovate.

PARAGRAPH 6:

a) Innovation is a process that you can use in everyday life.

b) Innovation is something that is best left to the experts.

E. What is the main idea of the reading?

_____

_____

F. Choose the word or phrase that best completes each sentence, according to the text.

1 Berkun dislikes the term innovation because he feels people use it too _____.

a) much   b) little   c) quickly

2 Innovation can happen in _____ ways.

    a) forgotten   b) few   c) many

3 Innovation is about solving problems in _____ ways.

    a) new   b) old   c) lost

4 The video camera and bucket of water were used to make _____ .

    a) money   b) bubbles   c) a point

5 The designer and the engineer were both innovators but had different _____ .

    a) buckets   b) roles   c) video cameras

6 Innovation can benefit from the work of _____ people.

    a) lazy   b) many   c) uncritical

FOCUS ON GRAMMAR

Simple Past Tense

Use the simple past tense when writing or talking about an action that began and ended in the past. You saw examples of the past tense in the previous reading in paragraph 4. To form the simple past tense of regular verbs add -*d*, -*ed*, or -*ied* to the base form of the verb (see the table below).

Example: After he **studied** at two universities in Europe, Tesla **worked** at a telephone company.

A. Here are three basic rules for forming the simple past tense of regular verbs. Follow the rules to complete the examples.

FOR VERBS ENDING IN …	SIMPLE PAST TENSE	EXAMPLES	
-*e*	add -*d*	achieve	*achieved*
		create	_____
a consonant + -*y*	change -*y* to -*i* and add -*ed*	apply	_____
		try	_____
anything else	add -*ed*	link	_____

B. Some of the most common verbs in English are irregular and don't follow these rules. Write each verb in the simple past tense. Work with a partner. Look up the ones you don't know.

BASE VERB	SIMPLE PAST TENSE	BASE VERB	SIMPLE PAST TENSE
be	*was/were*	know	
do		make	
get		say	
go		see	
have	*had*	take	

My eLab 🖉

Visit My eLab to complete Grammar Review exercises for this chapter. Visit My eLab Documents to see the Irregular Verbs List.

What do Alexander Graham Bell, Marie Curie, Leonardo da Vinci, and the Wright brothers have in common? They were all innovators, using their understanding of science to make something new. We remember innovators because they change the world, making it better. Nikola Tesla (1856–1943) is an innovator who should be more famous.

VOCABULARY BUILD

In the following exercises, explore key words from Reading 2.

A. Choose the word in parentheses that best completes each sentence. Key words are in bold.

❶ Telsa's **relationship** with Edison was as (employee / friend) and employer.

❷ Tesla lost the **credit**, or (blame / acknowledgment), for his innovations.

❸ Telsa **created**, or (lost / built), a generator at Niagara Falls.

❹ The crowd **linked** arms so they were all (joined / separated).

B. The words *create*, *generate*, *destroy*, *link*, and *reject* are all verbs. Fill in the blanks to show the relationships between these words.

❶ *Create* is the antonym of _____.

❷ When you *destroy* something, you _____ it.

❸ A synonym for *create* is _____.

❹ One _____ among these words is that they are all *processes*.

C. What do the words in bold mean to you? Complete the sentences.

❶ What is something you have **created**?

I created _____

_____

❷ What is an idea you **rejected**?

I rejected _____

_____

❸ Who is your closest **relationship** with?

My closest relationship _____

_____

❹ What do you **link** to your success as a student?

I link _____

_____

❺ What is something good that you take **credit** for?

I take credit for _____

_____

Before You Read

A. There are two kinds of electrical power. One is Thomas Edison's *direct current* (DC), stored in batteries. The other is Nikola Tesla's greatest invention, *alternating current* (AC). Alternating current is used for everything from house lights to things you plug into a wall socket. It's also used for charging batteries. Look at these pictures and indicate which use AC and which use DC. Discuss with a partner.

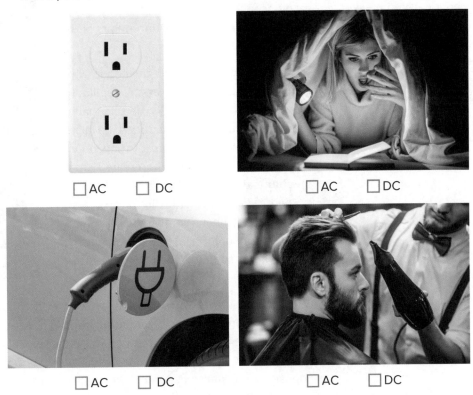

☐ AC   ☐ DC   ☐ AC   ☐ DC

☐ AC   ☐ DC   ☐ AC   ☐ DC

B. Reflect on what you know about Tesla and about electricity. Write three things you know and three questions you would like to know the answers to. After you read the text, return to this table and fill in the last column (What I Learned).

	WHAT I KNOW	MY QUESTIONS	WHAT I LEARNED
NIKOLA TELSA			
ELECTRICITY			

While You Read

C. While you read, reflect on the main idea of the reading.

Electric Dreams

Near Niagara Falls is a bronze statue of a seated man. He wears a long laboratory coat. He concentrates as he stares at a document in
5 his hands. His hands and feet shine brightly from so many people touching them. But many people may not know that the statue honours one of the greatest innovators of the 20th century, Nikola Tesla.

10 Tesla was born in 1856 and grew up in what is now Croatia. When he was still a child, he saw a picture of Niagara Falls. He said that he wanted to build a wheel that turned the falling water into power. His interest in inventions
15 came from his mother, who created small **mechanical tools** in their home. After he studied at two universities in Europe, Tesla worked at a telephone company. His attempts to interest people in his ideas for electric
20 motors failed so he decided to move to the United States.

After arriving in New York City, Tesla went to work for one of the greatest inventors in history, Thomas Edison. The **relationship** did not last long, and Tesla left to invent on his own. Tesla's greatest invention was the idea of alternating current (AC), which
25 is now used in most electric devices from light bulbs to washing machines. It was the opposite of Edison's version of direct current (DC), used in batteries. Edison did everything he could to destroy interest in Tesla's innovation. For example, at that time a new **electric chair** was introduced for executions. It used alternating current and Edison shared that fact to suggest alternating current was dangerous.

30 AC wasn't dangerous and, in 1893, the International Columbian Exhibition, held in Chicago, **rejected** Edison's DC lights. Instead, Tesla's AC lights were used for the first time on a big scale. Two years later, in 1895, Tesla achieved his childhood dream and **created** the world's first **hydroelectric power generating** station using the falling water of Niagara Falls. The electricity was used to power lights in the nearby city of
35 Buffalo, New York. Soon, Tesla's lighting systems became popular in cities around the world. Tesla won his war of electrical standards with Edison.

However, life did not go smoothly for Tesla. He started many other interesting projects yet most of them failed. He went bankrupt and lost all his money. He was always working on new innovations so he often didn't find time to patent his creations.
40 Others got both the **credit** and the **profits**. Eventually, Tesla had a **nervous breakdown**. He died in 1943.

These days, the name Tesla is **linked** with another innovator, Elon Musk, and his line of electric cars. When you see a Tesla car—or other inventions you plug in the wall— you should remember the person behind them.

(457 words)

After You Read

D. Return to Before You Read, task B. Fill in the last column.

E. Here are the main ideas from each paragraph in Reading 2. Number them in order. Then write the main idea of the reading.

_____1_____ Nikola Tesla was one of the greatest innovators of the 20th century.

_____ Tesla experienced successes at the International Columbian Exhibition, the generating station at Niagara Falls, and the lighting of Buffalo, New York.

_____ Tesla worked with Edison but they became competitors.

_____ Tesla's early success did not continue because he only focused on his ideas.

_____ Tesla's influences included his mother and his university studies.

_____6_____ Tesla should be remembered as an inspiration.

The main idea of the reading is _____

_____

F. Based on your understanding of Reading 2, take this survey. Indicate how you feel about each statement. Then discuss your answers with a partner.

STATEMENTS	COMPLETELY AGREE		NEITHER AGREE OR DISAGREE		COMPLETELY DISAGREE
❶ Tesla should have stayed in Croatia.	1	2	3	4	5
❷ Tesla should have stayed at a university in Europe.	1	2	3	4	5
❸ Tesla should have accepted Edison's ideas.	1	2	3	4	5
❹ It's no surprise that Tesla became Edison's enemy.	1	2	3	4	5
❺ Tesla should not have started other projects.	1	2	3	4	5
❻ Tesla should have paid more attention to patents.	1	2	3	4	5
❼ Tesla should be more famous than Edison.	1	2	3	4	5

FOCUS ON
WRITING

Writing Compound Sentences

You already learned about simple sentences in Chapter 1 (page 9). Sometimes you want to express more complicated ideas. Simple sentences only need a subject and a verb to make a complete thought.

Examples: Tesla was born in 1856. Tesla grew up in what is now Croatia.
Tesla could not build his inventions. Tesla moved to the United States.

Compound sentences combine two thoughts with a conjunction—a joining word. Common conjunctions include *and, but, or,* and *so.*

Examples: Tesla was born in 1856 **and** he grew up in what is now Croatia.
Tesla could not build his inventions **so** he moved to the United States.

In these examples the second use of Tesla's name is replaced with the pronoun *he* to avoid repetition.

A. Rewrite these pairs of simple sentences to make compound sentences. Use the conjunction in parentheses and pronouns to avoid repetition.

① (and) The relationship did not last long. Tesla left to work on his own.

_____

_____

② (but) The designers were confused. The designers agreed.

_____

_____

③ (or) Remember Tesla when you see an electric car. Remember Tesla when you turn on a light bulb.

_____

_____

④ (so) Tesla was always working on electrical innovations. Tesla failed to find time to patent them.

_____

_____

B. Match these nouns to the pronouns that could replace them in a compound sentence.

NOUNS		PRONOUNS
① Tesla and Edison	_____	a) she
② Tesla's mother	_____	b) it
③ Thomas Edison	_____	c) we
④ an electric car	_____	d) he
⑤ you and I	_____	e) they

© **ERPI** • Reproduction prohibited

WARM-UP ASSIGNMENT
Describe an Innovation

In this Warm-Up Assignment you will describe an old innovation of your choice.

A. Decide which old innovation you will describe. Find and print an illustration or a photo of it. The innovation you choose should be different from what you would see today. Check with your teacher to be sure it is appropriate for the task.

For example, look at these two photos: an old steam train and a modern electric bullet train. You don't need to include a modern photo with your sentences but this example helps you spot what was different about old trains.

B. Write simple sentences in the past tense to describe the old innovation. (See Focus on Grammar, page 29.)

Example: The train **used** a steam-powered engine. The train **was slow**.

_____

_____

_____

C. Combine your simple sentences into compound sentences (see Focus on Writing). Use conjunctions (*and, but, or, so*) and pronouns to avoid repetition.

Example: The train used a steam-powered engine **but it** was slow.

_____

_____

_____

D. Check your sentences.

☐ Is your spelling and punctuation correct?

☐ Did you use the simple past tense?

☐ Did you write compound sentences with conjunctions and pronouns?

E. Read your sentences aloud. Are there any other errors?

F. Make corrections and write a final copy. Share your sentences with a partner.

Use feedback from your teacher and classmates on this Warm-Up Assignment to improve your writing.

Changing the World

Entrepreneur Jim Rohn (1930–2009) said, "You are the average of the five people you spend the most time with." You are influenced by those you are closest to, but you are also influenced by your generation—people born around the same time as you. The idea of a generation of people behaving alike started with the Baby Boomers, those born shortly after World War II. Which generation are you?

In the following exercises, explore key words from Reading 3.

A. Match each word to its definition.

WORDS		DEFINITIONS
❶ active (adj.)	_____	a) conclusions you draw
❷ financial (adj.)	_____	b) important assignment
❸ generation (n.)	_____	c) involved in something
❹ implications (n.)	_____	d) people of the same age
❺ mission (n.)	_____	e) relating to money

B. Words like *influence* and *launch* can be used as nouns or as verbs. Fill in the blanks to complete the sentences.

❶ I don't try to _____ my friend's decisions.

❷ The weather is perfect to _____ the boat.

❸ The biggest _____ in my life is my brother.

❹ The product _____ is taking place in the new café.

C. What do the words in bold mean to you? Complete the sentences.

❶ What is a popular pastime for your **generation**?

A popular pastime _____

_____

❷ Who is a big **influence** in your life?

A big influence _____

_____

❸ What sport or hobby are you **active** in?

I'm active in _____

_____

❹ Who would you ask for **financial** advice?

I would ask _____

_____

My eLab 🖉

Visit My eLab to complete Vocabulary Review exercises for this chapter.

Before You Read

A. Look at the chart. It shows generations from the Baby Boomers, born after World War II, to the Millennials, born between 1995 and 2004. Circle the generation that you were born into.

1950	**Baby Boomers** 1946-1965
1960	
1970	**Generation X** 1966-1976
1980	**Generation Y** 1977-1994
1990	
2000	**Millennials** 1995-2004

B. Reading 3 tells the story of two people who created innovations to try to help others. Kidogo offers early childhood education programs in Africa and Go2gether is a ride-sharing app. What is something innovative that you would like to do that could help others?

_____

_____

While You Read

C. While you read, think about what is most important to the two people in the reading. Write your answers here.

Afzal Habib: _____

_____

Alice Park: _____

_____

Changing the World

demographic cohort (n.): large group of people with similar characteristics

peak spending years (n.): when people have the most money

nagging reality (n.): uncomfortable time and place that you cannot avoid

sustainable (adj.): able to be maintained at a certain rate or level

Today's teenagers and young adults, a **demographic cohort** referred to as the Millennial Generation, make up roughly 25 percent of the North American population
5 and an estimated 2.5 billion global citizens. Arguably the largest living **generation** since the Baby Boomers, the economic and political **influence** of Millennials is growing as they enter or move through the workforce toward their **peak spending years**. Right behind them is Generation Z,
10 the **impact** of which we're just beginning to see.

For both, the Internet is an appendage, climate change is a **nagging reality**, mobility is just the way things are, and the weight of the future is on their shoulders. It's for this reason the United Nations says youth from around the world must be an **active** part of all levels of decision-making related to **sustainable** development. It affects
15 their lives today and has **implications** for their futures.

Afzal Habib

mentored (v.): advised

Afzal Habib had a six-figure salary at the Boston Consulting Group, where he advised Fortune 500 clients. But he was looking to inject more meaning into his work. Afzal quit his job in Canada, and moved to Africa. In just one year he turned his idea into Kidogo,
20 a thriving, fully functional social enterprise with twenty-two staff. The company's **mission** is to bring high quality, easy-to-access, and affordable early childhood development (ECD) programs to poor developing-world communities. It sets up full-service "hubs" in targeted communities that employ certified teachers and host up to eighty students. Those hubs, once embedded in a community, provide training, marketing, and curriculum support
25 for smaller, nearby villages. The first pilot hub in Nairobi broke even in less than a year.

> "To me, sustainability is core to running a successful business, not just something on the periphery."

Alice Park

Alice Park attended Simon Fraser University. She learned that students living in her
30 neighbourhood bought more than twenty-five university parking passes. "Why don't these people share a ride instead of driving separately?" she thought to herself. A year later, Alice co-founded Go2gether, a Vancouver-based technology start-up that has since developed a ride-sharing app. The company's mission is to **reduce** the number of single-occupancy vehicles on roads. Since its **launch**, Go2gether has created
35 more than twenty jobs and is being used on a trial basis by the university, an airport, and a **financial** co-op. Alice is an active carpooler. Her most memorable ride was a trip from Vancouver to Toronto with a guy named Chris—and his dog, Bruno. She has **mentored** over fifty aspiring social entrepreneurs and was a vice-curator of the World Economic Forum's Global Shaper Hub in Vancouver.

40　　　"I'm simply doing my part to shape economic transformation through sharing resources and building more resilient communities. I'm grateful that I'm not alone and I remain hopeful."

(456 words)

Corporate Knights. (2015, March 27). Meet the Canadian top 30 under 30. Retrieved from www.corporateknights. com/magazines/2015-youth-future-40-issue/meet-the-canadian-top-30-under-30-14274150/

After You Read

D. Connect the phrases to summarize Reading 3.

SUMMARY		
1 The economic and political influence ...	_____	a) related to sustainable development.
2 We are just beginning to see the ...	_____	b) is core to success.
3 The United Nations says youth must be an active part of the decision-making ...	_____	c) of Millennials is growing.
4 Afzal Habib was earning a lot of money but ...	_____	d) developed a ride-sharing app.
5 Habib thinks sustainability ...	_____	e) he wanted more meaning in his work.
6 Alice Park co-founded Go2gether and ...	_____	f) impact of Generation Z.

E. Indicate whether these statements are true or false, according to the text.

STATEMENTS	TRUE	FALSE
1 The Millennial Generation only make up 2.5 percent of the North American population.		
2 Millennials' peak spending years will be when they are earning high salaries.		
3 The idea that the Internet is an appendage (attachment) suggests Generation Z uses it all the time.		
4 Afzal Habib quit his job in Africa and moved to Canada.		
5 Kidogo provides early childhood development (ECD) programs in Africa.		
6 Go2gether's success is measured in the number of jobs it created and interest from other organizations.		

Academic
Survival Skill

Remembering What You Learn

When you study, you need to remember a lot of information. It helps if you read with a purpose, if you know why something is important to you. Thinking in pictures and describing things are two other techniques that can help you remember what you learn.

A. Use all your senses. Think about what you see, hear, smell, taste, and feel. If you are reading about a place or looking at a picture, it helps to imagine you are there.

For example, look at this picture of Niagara Falls where Nikola Tesla built the first hydro-electric power plant. You may not be able to use all your senses, but what would you experience if you were there?

SEE: _____

HEAR: _____

SMELL: _____

TASTE: _____

FEEL: _____

B. It also helps to think about how things work. You can find or draw diagrams to help you remember. Here is a diagram of a dam used to make electricity. Number the steps in order to create a description of how it works.

_____ The water flows into the river.

_____ Some of the water flows through the dam and turns giant blades.

_____ The dam turns part of a river into a lake.

_____ The turning of the blades creates electricity.

C. Look at the two images again. Did they help you remember details? Which of your senses will you try to use more in the future?

FINAL ASSIGNMENT
Write a Descriptive Paragraph

Use what you learned in this chapter to write a paragraph that describes an old innovation.

A. Build on your Warm-Up Assignment to write a draft of your paragraph. Organize the sentences in a logical order. Start with a topic sentence, the main idea of your paragraph (see Focus on Reading, page 24).

B. Write both simple and compound sentences (Focus on Writing, page 34) in the simple past tense (Focus on Grammar, page 29). When writing the compound sentences, use conjunctions (*and, but, or, so*) and pronouns to avoid repetition.

C. Think about what you learned in Academic Survival Skill: use all your senses when you write details.

D. You received feedback on your Warm-Up Assignment from your teacher and classmates. Use this feedback to consider how you can improve your writing.

E. Refer to the Models Chapter (page 165) to see an example of a descriptive paragraph and to learn more about how to write one.

F. Proofread your paragraph. Use the checklist from the Warm-Up Assignment.

G. Read your paragraph aloud. Are there any other errors? Make corrections and write a final copy. Share your paragraph with a partner.

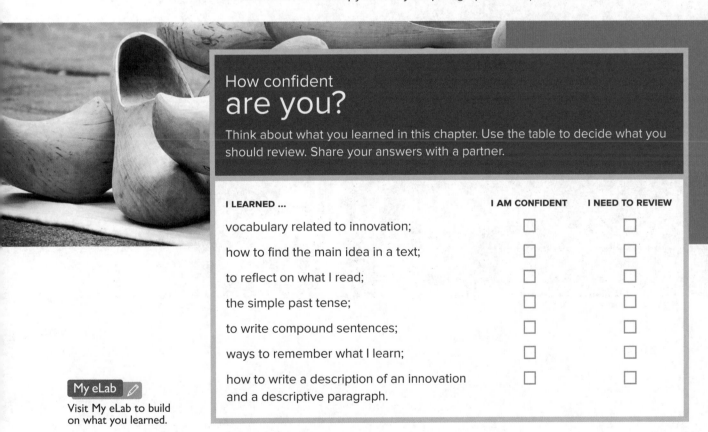

How confident
are you?

Think about what you learned in this chapter. Use the table to decide what you should review. Share your answers with a partner.

I LEARNED ...	I AM CONFIDENT	I NEED TO REVIEW
vocabulary related to innovation;	☐	☐
how to find the main idea in a text;	☐	☐
to reflect on what I read;	☐	☐
the simple past tense;	☐	☐
to write compound sentences;	☐	☐
ways to remember what I learn;	☐	☐
how to write a description of an innovation and a descriptive paragraph.	☐	☐

My eLab ✎
Visit My eLab to build on what you learned.

CHAPTER 3

Finding Success

What leads to success? What leads to failure? In business, success is often measured by how much a company is worth, how large it grows, and how it stretches around the world. But there are other measures of success. For businesses and individuals, one measure is innovation—looking at needs or problems and creating products and services that others want to use. It can be difficult to be an innovator but, if you are successful, the rewards can be huge. Is there a secret formula to business success?

In this chapter, you will

- learn vocabulary related to success;
- identify supporting details;
- ask follow-up questions;
- use conjunctions to write sentences;
- review the past progressive tense;
- learn how to manage time;
- write a chronological list and a chronological paragraph.

GEARING UP

A. Look at a business earnings line chart. Earnings are how much money a business makes. Think about a new restaurant and then answer the questions.

Business Earnings over Time

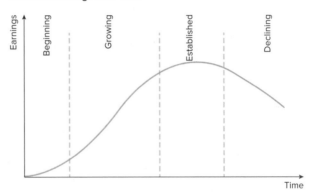

1 Why are earnings slow, at first, at a new restaurant?

_____

_____

2 The growing stage has high earnings. How does a restaurant grow?

_____

_____

3 When a restaurant is established, earnings are the highest. Why don't earnings go higher?

_____

_____

4 What makes a restaurant decline and earnings fall?

_____

_____

B. Discuss the questions and your answers with a partner.

Below are the key words you will practise in this chapter. Check the words you understand and then underline the words you use.

context
contract
cycle
environment
evidence
rights
schedules

nouns

abandon
contributed
establish
reduce
responded
share

verbs

success

adjectives
annual
common
complex
professional
traditional
unique

adverb — internationally

preposition — despite

These words are from the Longman Communication 3000 and the Academic Word List. See Appendix 1, page 172.

Identifying Supporting Details

FOCUS ON READING

In Chapter 2, you learned how to identify the main idea in a paragraph and in a text. Supporting details provide additional information that develop and support the main idea. Here are four ways to identify supporting details.

• Read the first and the last sentence to find the main idea in a paragraph.
• Read the first and the last paragraph to find the main idea in a text.
• Look for numbers and for words that are capitalized.
• Look for examples and explanations.

Read this excerpt from Reading 1. Then answer the questions.

Veuve Clicquot is pronounced "vuv kliko."

> No one expected Barbe-Nicole Ponsardin to become a successful business-woman. When she was twenty-one, she married François Clicquot, the son of another wealthy family. Six years later, in 1805, François died and Barbe-Nicole became Veuve (widow) Clicquot. She was not poor: her husband had left her banking, wool, and champagne businesses. But Veuve Clicquot decided that champagne would be her only business. Soon, she was inventing new ways to make champagne. By the time she died, in 1866, Veuve Clicquot's champagne company was a world leader.

1 Read the first and the last sentence. Write the main idea of the paragraph.

_____

_____

2 Read the excerpt again and underline numbers and words that are capitalized.

3 Highlight the examples and the explanations.

Asking Follow-up Questions

When you read, think of questions you want answered. Sometimes your questions are answered later, as you continue to read. Sometimes you may need to look for more information. Common questions start with *who, what, when, where, why,* and *how.*

A. Read this excerpt from Reading 1. Then read the questions. Can you answer any of them? Discuss with a partner.

Where is the Mattel business located?

Why did her daughter prefer adult dolls?

How did Handler design Barbie?

> Since women often spend more time with children, they sometimes create businesses because of them. One day, Ruth Handler was watching her daughter play with paper cut-out dolls and she noticed that she preferred the ones that looked like adults. In 1959, Handler invented the unique Barbie doll. It became popular. In five years, her and her husband's company—Mattel—was a multi-million dollar business. Barbie dolls still generate a billion dollars in annual earnings.

Who was Barbie named after?

What else does Mattel sell?

When did Barbie become a big seller?

B. Read this excerpt from Reading 2. Fill in the blanks with *who, what, when, where, why* or *how* to complete the questions. Can you guess the answers to any of these questions? Discuss with a partner.

> William Henry Gates III was born in 1955. His father was a lawyer and his mother was a schoolteacher, in Seattle. Twelve years later, in 1967, Gates became a private school student. After Gates started, the school bought an early computer. Gates was starting to learn programming when he got his first professional programming job. It was to create a computerized class schedule.

1 _____ did Gates start learning programming?

2 _____ did the school get a computer?

3 _____ in Seattle was the school?

4 _____ old was Gates when he graduated?

5 _____ was Gates' teacher?

6 _____ was the name of Gates' school?

READING 1   A Woman's Business

In the past, most women worked, but few were business leaders. One reason was that women did not have the same educational opportunities as men. But many women became leaders anyway. Often they created new business opportunities. Today, there are more women running successful businesses.

In the following exercises, explore key words from Reading 1.

A. Fill in the blanks with the correct words to complete the sentences.

common	environment	internationally	share

1 Business success is often at the expense of the _____.

2 Women have different opportunities to succeed _____.

3 A _____ problem for women is getting money to start a business.

4 Some women _____ their skills to start a new business.

B. Read each sentence and use the context to help you define the word in bold. Use a dictionary to check your answers.

1 In 1959, she invented the **unique** Barbie doll.

_____

2 Barbie dolls still generate a billion dollars in **annual** earnings for Mattel.

_____

3 It was the first perfume that was **internationally** popular.

_____

4 She provided **traditional** cures to take care of women.

_____

C. What do the words in bold mean to you? Complete the sentences.

1 What is an **annual** event?

An annual event is _____

2 What is a **traditional** business?

A traditional business is _____

_____

3 What is the name of a restaurant you might **share** with friends?

I might share _____

4 What is a **common** type of business?

A common type of business is _____

5 What is a **unique** business you know?

A unique business I know is _____

6 What do you do to help the **environment**?

To help the environment, I _____

_____

Before You Read

A. Think of three women you know who work. What businesses do they work in? Which roles do they have? Fill in the mind map and then discuss it with a partner.

| ROLE: *owner* | BUSINESS: *coffee shop* |
| ROLE: | BUSINESS: |

A WOMAN'S BUSINESS

| BUSINESS: | ROLE: |
| BUSINESS: | ROLE: |

B. Scan the first and last paragraph to get the main idea of the reading.

While You Read

C. While you read, underline supporting details and circle dates, numbers, and words that are capitalized (except for words that begin a sentence).

A Woman's Business

champagne (n.): kind of wine

home remedies (n.): traditional cures

cosmetics (n.): make-up to improve one's appearance

perspective (n.): point of view

No one expected Barbe-Nicole Ponsardin to become a successful businesswoman. When she was twenty-one, she married François Clicquot, the son of another wealthy family. Six years later, in 1805, François died, and Barbe-Nicole became Veuve (widow)
5 Clicquot. She was not poor: her husband had left her banking, wool, and **champagne** businesses. But Veuve Clicquot decided that champagne would be her only business. Soon, she was inventing new ways to make champagne. By the time she died, in 1866, Veuve Clicquot's champagne company was a world leader.

Clicquot's story is **common**. Before her, many women were running family businesses.
10 Many more started new businesses, often based on what they knew from other women. For example, in 1875, the American Lydia Estes Pinkham understood women's health issues and was making **home remedies**, but she expanded the sale of these **traditional** cures to create a national business.

Coco Chanel
(1883–1971)

While Pinkham dealt with women's needs, Coco Chanel helped
15 women with their desires. In 1910, Chanel opened a shop to sell women's hats. In 1921, she came up with Chanel No. 5, the first perfume that was **internationally** popular. Many women started clothing and **cosmetics** businesses after Chanel's success.

Since women often spend more time with children, they
20 sometimes create businesses because of them. One day, Ruth Handler was watching her daughter play with paper cut-out dolls and she noticed that she preferred the dolls that looked like adults. In 1959, Handler created the **unique** Barbie doll. It became popular. Within five years, her and her husband's
25 company—Mattel—was a multi-million dollar business. Barbie dolls still generate a billion dollars in **annual** earnings.

Sometimes women start businesses with a different **perspective** than businesses owned by men. England's Anita Roddick founded The Body Shop, in 1976. It sells cosmetics, but when Roddick was travelling
30 around the world, she met a lot of underpaid workers. She used the principle of fair trade to **share** profits with workers. She also decided that her stores and products should be good for the **environment**.

Women now work in all areas of business. One example is Chinese businesswoman Zhou Qunfei. Before she was born, her father went blind. Her mother died when she
35 was five. She became a **migrant worker** in Shenzhen. Soon, she was attending a nearby university, even though she had dropped out of school. She studied many different courses. In 2003, she set up a company making touch screens. She started with nothing but her business became worth $10 billion.

Today, every business is women's business.

(411 words)

After You Read

D. Choose the phrase that best completes each sentence.

1. A home remedies business to improve women's health is an example of _____.

   a) a business that cannot grow

   b) a business that operates locally

   c) understanding women's needs

2. Coco Chanel's perfume became _____.

   a) an international phenomenon

   b) popular in the south of France

   c) less popular than her hats

3. Ruth Handler's success was because she noticed her daughter's _____.

   a) interest in business

   b) preference for adult dolls

   c) interest in education

4. Anita Roddick's fair trade business decisions were based on _____.

   a) earning more money

   b) business strategies

   c) meeting workers

5. The story of Zhou Qunfei shows that women can be successful _____.

   a) despite big challenges

   b) by avoiding university

   c) by being a billionaire

6. The phrase "every business is women's business" means _____.

   a) men are no longer in business

   b) men and women want different things

   c) women can start and lead any business

E. Match each businesswoman to her secret to success.

BUSINESSWOMEN		SECRET TO SUCCESS
1. Barbe-Nicole Ponsardin	_____	a) used fair trade business practices
2. Lydia Estes Pinkham	_____	b) focused on one business
3. Coco Chanel	_____	c) continued to learn
4. Ruth Handler	_____	d) watched her daughter's behaviour
5. Anita Roddick	_____	e) created an international brand
6. Zhou Qunfei	_____	f) worked with one group of customers

Using Conjunctions to Write Sentences

Conjunctions are words that connect two words, phrases, or sentences. The most common conjunctions are *and*, *but*, *or*.

Examples: We travelled **and** worked.
We travelled **but** did not work.
We travelled **or** worked.

Other conjunctions, like *because*, show a reason. These and other conjunctions can connect two parts—or *clauses*—of a sentence.

Example: We travelled **because** we worked in different cities.

A. Some conjunctions show relationships in time. Write these words in the correct place on the timeline: *after, before, until*.

_____ _____ ← **now** → *when, while* _____

B. Underline the conjunction in each sentence.

① She married when she was twenty-one.

② While Pinkham dealt with women's needs, Coco Chanel helped with their desires.

③ Women sometimes think about children's needs because they spend more time with them.

④ After Coco Chanel's success, many women started similar businesses.

⑤ Zhou Qunfei attended university when she moved to Shenzhen.

C. Use the conjunction in parentheses to connect each pair of sentences.

① (because) IBM needed software. IBM developed a new personal computer.

IBM needed software because it developed a new personal computer. _____

② (when) Paul Allen became sick. Bill Gates took over Microsoft.

_____

_____

③ (while) Gates was going to Harvard University. He made money with programming languages.

_____

_____

④ (after) Gates married Melinda French. They started a foundation.

_____

_____

⑤ (because) Gates saw the need for photo sharing. He started Corbis.

_____

_____

READING ②   A Billionaire Dropout

A common measure of success is how much money a business or its owner makes. For a long time, Bill Gates was the richest person in the world. But now Gates thinks success is about how he spends his money to help others. What is more important to success: making money or spending it?

VOCABULARY BUILD

In the following exercises, explore key words from Reading 2.

A. Many words have different meanings and parts of speech. Fill in the blanks with the correct words to complete each pair of sentences.

cycle	professional	rights	schedule

① I need a _____ to get all my work done.

Can you _____ a meeting for next Thursday?

② I need exercise, so I _____ to work.

A business _____ can include starting, growing, and failing.

③ A common business _____ is a lawyer.

You need to be _____ to be respected in business.

④ Every business should know its legal _____.

To get to the bank, follow this street then take three _____.

B. Draw an arrow ↓ to indicate where the word in parentheses should be placed in each sentence.

① (contract) He wanted a before he agreed to start working there .

② (establish) She wanted to a company that would help poor women .

③ (contributed) We all money to help start the new business .

C. What do the words in bold mean to you? Complete the sentences.

① What do you want to do for your **professional** career?

For my professional career, I want to _____

_____

② What is on your **schedule** this weekend?

On my schedule this weekend _____

_____

③ What kind of company would you like to **establish**?

A company I would like to establish _____

_____

④ What was something you **contributed** recently?

Something I contributed recently _____

_____

⑤ What is one of your **rights** as a student?

One of my rights as a student _____

_____

Before You Read

A. Reading 2 is about Bill Gates. Discuss with a partner what you already know about Gates. Take notes below.

```
┌─────────────────────────────────────────────────────────┐
│                                                         │
│                                                         │
│                                                         │
│                                                         │
│                                                         │
│                                                         │
│                                                         │
│                                                         │
└─────────────────────────────────────────────────────────┘
```

B. Self-made billionaires are people who make their money; they do not get it from relatives. In 2013, *Forbes Magazine* listed how 227 self-made billionaires made their money. Circle what you think is the most common way to become a billionaire. Underline what you think is the least common way. Share your answers with a partner.

sports   food and beverages

health care

fashion and retail   **media**

energy   real estate

technology   **investments**

C. Write three questions you expect will be answered about Bill Gates in the text. Use *who, what, when, where, why*, or *how* words to start your questions.

_____

_____

_____

_____

While You Read

D. Use what you learned in Focus on Reading (page 44) to identify supporting details in the text.

A Billionaire Dropout

programming languages
(n.): codes computers use
to solve problems

**Chief Executive Officer
(CEO)** (n.): person in charge
of a company

honorary degree (n.): given
as a symbolic award by
a university

unfolded (v.): happened
in some way

dropouts (n.): people who
gave up on their studies

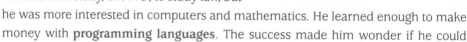

William Henry Gates III was born in 1955.
His father was a lawyer and his mother was
a schoolteacher, in Seattle. Twelve years later,
5 in 1967, Gates became a private school
student. After Gates started, the school
bought an early computer. Gates was starting
to learn programming when he got his first
professional programming job. It was to
10 create computerized class **schedules**.

Gates was a good student. He was going to
Harvard University, in 1973, to study law, but
he was more interested in computers and mathematics. He learned enough to make
money with **programming languages**. The success made him wonder if he could
15 **establish** his own company. In 1976, he took time off from Harvard to start Microsoft
with Paul Allen, a school friend. A year later, Gates was taking another break from
Harvard when he decided to drop out. Two years later, Microsoft was already earning
more than $1 million a year.

In 1981, Microsoft bought a disk operating system that became known by its acronym,
20 DOS. At that time, the computer company IBM was making a new personal computer.
IBM needed software to run it. Microsoft got the **contract** to build IBM's operating
system.

Two years after that, Gates had to take over full management of Microsoft when his
friend Allen became ill. By 1987, Gates was the youngest billionaire in history. It was
25 also the year he met his future wife, Melinda French.

By 1989, Gates realized that content would be increasingly important for computers,
so he founded the online company Corbis. Corbis sells **rights** to illustrations,
photographs, and video clips. In 1994, Gates and French married and soon had three
children.

30 Gates was making a lot of money and, a year later, in 1995, at age thirty-nine, Gates
became the world's richest man. People thought Gates should retire to enjoy his
money. Five years later, in 2000, Gates stepped away from his position as **Chief
Executive Officer** at Microsoft. He formed the Bill and Melinda Gates Foundation.

Gates never graduated from Harvard but, in 2007, he was given an **honorary degree**.
35 In 2014, he was interviewed by the magazine *Rolling Stone* and said, "It's pretty
amazing to go from a world where computers were unheard of, and very complex,
to where they're a tool of everyday life. That was the dream that I wanted to make
come true, and in a large part, it's **unfolded** as I'd expected."

Unlike most university **dropouts**, Gates has nothing to regret. (416 words)

References

Goodell, J. (2013, March 13). Bill Gates: The *Rolling Stone* interview. *Rolling Stone*. Retrieved from http://
www.rollingstone.com/culture/news/bill-gates-the-rolling-stone-interview-20140313

Kreit, A. and Wanke, J. (n.d.). Bill Gates, from geek to gazillionaire to do-gooder. *NPR, Timeline*. Retrieved
from http://www.npr.org/news/graphics/2008/june/bill_gates/gates_timeline_04.html

After You Read

E. Indicate whether these statements are true or false, according to the text.

STATEMENTS	TRUE	FALSE
1 Bill Gates' family was poor.		
2 Gates' parents were both teachers.		
3 There was a computer at Gates' school.		
4 Poor grades made Gates drop out of university.		
5 Gates started Microsoft with a school friend.		
6 Gates never expected for his life to turn out the way it did.		

F. Supporting details may be indicated by pronouns: words that take the place of nouns. Read the sentences and write *what* or *who* each word in bold refers to.

1 **He** was a lawyer and **she** was a schoolteacher. _____

2 **It** purchased an early computer. _____

3 **He** met Gates at school and they started Microsoft. _____

4 Gates dropped out of **it** to start Microsoft. _____

5 **She** married Gates in 1987. _____

G. Read what you wrote about Gates in Before You Read, task A, and your three questions from task C. Do you think Gates is a success? Why or why not?

_____

_____

_____

FOCUS ON GRAMMAR

Simple Past and Past Progressive Tenses

In Chapter 2, you learned about the simple past. You use the simple past to write about something that began and ended in the past. Sometimes you need to write about something that was in progress at a specific time in the past. Use the past progressive tense. The simple past and past progressive tenses are often used together. The past progressive can show what was happening when another action interrupted it.

PAST PROGRESSIVE	SIMPLE PAST	SIMPLE PAST AND PAST PROGRESSIVE
Gates **was learning** programming.	He **started** his first job.	Gates **was learning** programming when he **started** his first job.
They **were climbing** the mountain.	The weather **changed**.	They **were climbing** the mountain before the weather **changed**.

A. Fill in the blanks with the past progressive form of the verb in parentheses.

1 When he was young, Gates (create) _____*was creating*_____ a school schedule.

2 When they started Microsoft, Gates and his friend (take) _____ a break from Harvard.

3 IBM (invent) _____ a new personal computer in 1981.

4 Many companies (try) _____ to make software for IBM, at that time.

5 Gates (study) _____ at university before he started his business.

6 Gates (dream) _____ about the future, when IBM offered him a job.

7 Gates (make) _____ a lot of money and, by the age of thirty-nine, was the world's richest man.

8 By 1989, Gates (realize) _____ that content would become important for computers.

B. Rewrite these sentences. Change the verb tense from the simple past to the past progressive. Remember to use *was* or *were*.

1 After 1805, she **invented** new ways to make champagne.

   After 1805, she was inventing new ways to make champagne.

2 Before her, many women **ran** family businesses.

   _____

   _____

3 In 1921, Coco Chanel **helped** women with their desires.

   _____

   _____

4 One day, Ruth Handler **watched** her daughter play with paper cut-out dolls.

   _____

   _____

5 When Roddick **travelled** around the world, she met a lot of underpaid workers.

   _____

   _____

6 Zhou Qunfei **attended** a nearby university when she lived in Shenzhen.

   _____

   _____

My eLab

Visit My eLab to complete Grammar Review exercises for this chapter.

WARM-UP ASSIGMNENT
Write a List of Events

Reading 2 talked about Bill Gates' dates and the things he was doing. In this Warm-Up Assignment, write your own biography with dates. Use the simple past and past progressive tenses.

A. Write your list of events below. Start with the year you were born. List six events. Events and accomplishments can include graduations, participation in sports or other activities, awards, trips, or other events that impacted your life.

B. Write about what was happening at that time using the past progressive tense you learned in Focus on Grammar (page 53). Connect the events and things that were happening with conjunctions you learned in Focus on Writing (page 49).

Example:

years	1997	I **was born** in Hong Kong. ⟵——————— *simple past tense*
	2001	I **went** to school while my parents **were working**. ⟵—— *simple past and past progressive tense*
	2017	I was travelling **before** I started university. ⟵ *conjunction*

YEAR   **EVENT**

_____   _____

_____   _____

_____   _____

_____   _____

_____   _____

_____   _____

C. Check your spelling and grammar. Did you use the simple past and past progressive tenses? Did you connect them with conjunctions?

D. Write your final list. Refer to the Models Chapter (page 164) to see an example of a chronological list and to learn more about how to write one.

E. Compare lists in a group. Use question words to ask other students about their events: *who, what, when, where, why,* and *how.*

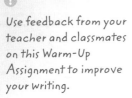

Use feedback from your teacher and classmates on this Warm-Up Assignment to improve your writing.

We're Wrong

Business uses many metaphors—ideas and images that symbolize something else. A popular metaphor is a mountain. Climbing a mountain is difficult and sometimes dangerous, but it can be done in different ways. In Reading 3, Tony Crabbe uses a mountain metaphor to write about how businesses and people can fail.

VOCABULARY BUILD

In the following exercises, explore key words from Reading 3.

A. Choose the word in parentheses that best completes each sentence. Key words are in bold.

❶ **Despite** wanting to climb the mountain, Ahmed chose (not to / to) go.

❷ The weather **evidence** suggested rain so she (didn't take / took) an umbrella.

❸ He wanted to **reduce** his work, so he (found / dropped) a partner.

❹ He wasn't ready to **abandon** the race, so he (stopped / continued).

B. Fill in the blanks to complete the sentences.

complex	context	responded

❶ When I called him, he _____ immediately.

❷ The business _____ is strong competition from others.

❸ She always looked busy because she had to do several different _____ tasks.

C. What do the words in bold mean to you? Complete the sentences.

❶ I read words in **context** to _____

_____

❷ I **respond** to the teacher's questions because _____

_____

❸ I sometimes waste time **despite** _____

_____

❹ When I see a **complex** problem, I _____

_____

❺ Something I need to **reduce** is _____

_____

❻ I would never **abandon** my _____

_____

My eLab ✎

Visit My eLab to complete Vocabulary Review exercises for this chapter.

Before You Read

A. Read the first paragraph of Reading 3 (page 58) and then write *who, what, when, where, why,* and *how* questions. Compare your questions with a partner. Can you guess any of the answers?

Who *were the climbers?* _____

What _____

When _____

Where _____

Why _____

How _____

B. Read the first and last sentence in paragraph 1 and write the main idea.

PARAGRAPH 1: _____

_____

C. Reading 3 focuses on the idea of being busy. Does being busy make you more successful? What are some advantages and disadvantages of being busy? Fill in the table and then discuss with a partner.

ADVANTAGES	DISADVANTAGES
You can avoid boredom.	*You may ignore important things.*

While You Read

D. Write the main ideas for paragraphs 2, 3, and 4. Then underline the supporting details.

PARAGRAPH 2: _____

_____

PARAGRAPH 3: _____

_____

PARAGRAPH 4: _____

_____

We're Wrong

summit (n.): peak or top of a mountain

frustrated (adj.): upset at being unable to do something

stockbroker (n.): someone who buys and sells investments for others

dispassionately (adv.): without emotion

agenda (n.): list of items to accomplish

frantically (adv.): quickly, in an upset or fearful way

In 1996, eight climbers set off to climb Everest. They had all the right equipment, they were well trained and they were fit. They made good progress. Then things changed. It appears there was something of a traffic jam toward the **summit**, and
5 there may have been some weather changes and so progress slowed. There is a rule on Everest that if you don't reach the summit by a certain time, you have to **abandon** your attempt. On that day, these really experienced but **frustrated** climbers should have turned back, but instead they kept going. They reached the summit too late in the day, had to climb down in darkness, and died.

10 Christopher Cave, a former **stockbroker**, heard about this and it bothered him. It reminded him of what he'd seen happen in a lot of companies. Those companies would commit to a strategy. Then, as the business **context** changed, evidence would start appearing that the strategy was a bad idea. Instead of looking **dispassionately** at the new information and stopping to reflect on a better course of action, these

15 businesses **responded** to their frustrated efforts with more activity. In effect, to avoid having to face the possibility that they were heading in the wrong direction, they increased their efforts in the wrong
20 direction.

I see the same thing with individuals. The world has changed. The problem is, we haven't. **Despite** all our technology and training, our strategies for coping and
25 succeeding come from the industrial age. They haven't changed, despite the **evidence** piling up that they're not working. Despite everything we try, we remain overloaded at work and **overcommitted** at home, and
30 it seems to be getting worse. Instead of facing the reality that our current approach doesn't seem to be helping **reduce** our sense of overwhelm, we redouble our efforts in the wrong direction, killing ourselves with endless busyness.

Busy is the easy option. We are busy because we don't make the tough choices. We allow the world and our inbox to set our **agenda**, rather than think for ourselves. It's
35 easier to simply react; to choose to try to do everything, rather than make the difficult decisions and unchoose things—it takes more courage to do less. In fact, as Ben Hunnicutt explains, busy is actually one of the seven deadly sins; it is slothfulness. In the Middle Ages, slothfulness had two forms: one was lazy, the other—called acedia—was running about **frantically**. "There is no real place I'm going, but I'm
40 making great time getting there."

(425 words)

Crabbe, T. (2015). *Busy: How to thrive in a world of too much* (pp. xv–xvii). New York: Grand Central Publishing.

After You Read

E. Connect the phrases to summarize Reading 3.

SUMMARY		
❶ Eight mountain climbers ...	_____	a) they continue on the same path.
❷ Many companies refuse to accept ...	_____	b) don't have to make tough choices.
❸ Instead of considering new information, ...	_____	c) refused to give up and died.
❹ Individuals still use strategies that ...	_____	d) running around frantically.
❺ Despite being overwhelmed, ...	_____	e) were successful in the industrial age.
❻ It's easy to be busy because you ...	_____	f) that business conditions may change.
❼ One form of slothfulness is ...	_____	g) individuals try to be busier.

F. Choose the word that best completes each sentence.

❶ Turning back from a goal is sometimes the _____ decision.

    a) worst   b) weakest   c) best

❷ It was not necessary for the climbers to _____.

    a) die   b) return   c) ski

❸ Christopher Cave was concerned about people who don't change their _____.

    a) lives   b) interests   c) strategies

❹ Companies often want to avoid the possibility they are heading in the _____ direction.

    a) wrong   b) right   c) easiest

❺ Most people have too many _____ at home.

    a) possessions   b) commitments   c) strategies

G. The theme of this chapter is success. Look at the main ideas you wrote for each paragraph in While You Read, task D. Then, in your own words, write the main idea of the reading.

_____

_____

_____

_____

_____

Academic
Survival Skill

Managing Your Time

Do you wish you had more time? Before college or university, teachers and parents probably helped you manage your time. But to succeed in your studies, you need to develop your own schedule and study habits. How can managing your time help you succeed?

A. How do you study? Indicate which tasks you already do and which you need to do.

TASKS	ALREADY DO	NEED TO DO
❶ Set regular times to study on a calendar.		
❷ Plan weekly reviews on a calendar.		
❸ Find a study partner to discuss what I'm learning.		
❹ Write my assignment due dates on a calendar.		
❺ Write test and exam due dates on a calendar.		

B. Look at the pictures. What times and places can you study? What ways can you study? Write your answers. Then discuss with a partner.

_____

_____

_____

_____

_____

> ❗ _Make a weekly schedule for homework and studying._

C. This table can help you decide what to do and when to do it. Write one task in each box. After, discuss in a group.

❶ URGENT AND IMPORTANT: DO IT NOW.	❷ IMPORTANT BUT NOT URGENT: DECIDE WHEN TO DO IT.
_____ _____	_____ _____
❸ URGENT BUT NOT IMPORTANT: GET OTHERS TO DO IT.	❹ NOT IMPORTANT AND NOT URGENT: IGNORE.
_____ _____	_____ _____

FINAL ASSIGNMENT
Write a Chronological Paragraph

The word *chronos* is Greek for *time*. A chronological paragraph explains events using times or dates. Use what you learned in this chapter to write a chronological paragraph.

A. Use your list from the Warm-Up Assignment to write a draft of your paragraph. In the Warm-Up Assignment, you followed the example,

> 1997   I was born in Hong Kong.

As the first sentence in your paragraph, you could write this as,

> I was born in 1997, in Hong Kong.

B. Continue writing using the simple past tense for events and adding conjunctions and the past progressive for details (refer to Focus on Grammar, page 53 and Focus on Writing, page 49).

> Examples: I went to school in 2001, while my parents were working.
>   In 2017, I was travelling before I started university.

C. You received feedback on your Warm-Up Assignment from your teacher and classmates. Use this feedback to consider how you can improve your writing.

D. Refer to the Models Chapter (page 165) to see an example of a chronological paragraph and to learn more about how to write one.

E. Proofread your paragraph. Check your spelling and grammar. Make corrections and write a final copy.

How confident are you?

Think about what you learned in this chapter. Use the table to decide what you should review. Share your answers with a partner.

I LEARNED ...	I AM CONFIDENT	I NEED TO REVIEW
vocabulary related to success;	☐	☐
to identify supporting details;	☐	☐
to ask follow-up questions;	☐	☐
how to use conjunctions to write sentences;	☐	☐
the past progressive tense;	☐	☐
how to manage time;	☐	☐
how to write a chronological list and a chronological paragraph.	☐	☐

My eLab 🖊

Visit My eLab to build on what you learned.

CHAPTER 4
Disrupting Business

In the 19th century, textile workers protested against machines that were taking over their jobs. Faster and cheaper steam-powered machines disrupted—or changed—industry. Today, many innovators are disrupting old businesses. Innovators use social media and the Internet to find faster and cheaper ways to do things. How will new technologies disrupt today's jobs? How will they affect your job?

In this chapter,
you will

- learn vocabulary related to business;

- scan for specific information;

- look for examples;

- use the possessive form;

- review how to write simple messages;

- learn ways to boost your vocabulary;

- write an informal message and a formal email.

GEARING UP

A. Look at the illustration and then answer the questions.

Waves of Digital Disruption

1995+
Music
Photography
Video rentals
...

2010+
TV
News
Travel
...

2015+
Retail
Healthcare
Finance
Cars
Education
...

...

1 1995+: Buying music online became more popular than buying physical recordings. Do you prefer buying music online? Why?

_____

_____

2 2010+: Instead of paying for newspapers, more people started getting their news online for free. How do news organizations make money?

_____

_____

3 2015+: Uber is the world's largest taxi company, but it doesn't own any cars. How does it make money?

_____

_____

4 THE FUTURE: Name another business that you think will soon change.

_____

B. Discuss the questions and your answers with a partner.

Below are the key words you will practise in this chapter. Check the words you understand and then underline the words you use.

These words are from the Longman Communication 3000 and the Academic Word List. See Appendix 1, page 172.

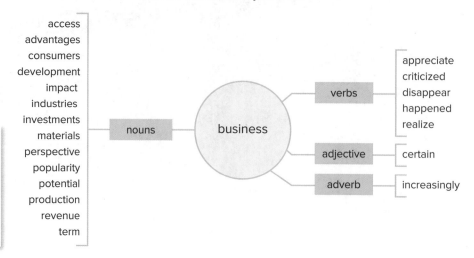

access
advantages
consumers
development
impact
industries
investments
materials
perspective
popularity
potential
production
revenue
term

nouns

business

verbs
appreciate
criticized
disappear
happened
realize

adjective
certain

adverb
increasingly

Scanning for Specific Information

Skimming and scanning are two important reading strategies. When you skim, you look at a text quickly to get a general idea of the content. When you scan, you look at a text to find specific information. Here are three ways to scan a text.

- Scan for key words and their synonyms. If you are looking for information about a *business*, you might also look for words about *companies*, *corporations*, and *industries*.

- Check headings and numbered points for the information you are looking for.

- Use your finger or a pen to move through the text, stopping at the information you need.

A. Scan this excerpt from Reading 2 and highlight the dates.

> Disruptive technologies' impact on education continues. In 1840, the new British postal service led to the development of correspondence courses. By 1938, hundreds of universities used radio to teach courses. In 1953, a university in Texas offered TV's first university course. And, in 1989, the University of Phoenix's Bachelor's and Master's degree courses started online, using the Internet.

B. Scan this excerpt from Reading 1 and underline words related to travel.

> In 1995, Harvard University's Clayton Christensen was the first to use the term *disruptive innovation*. He used the term to explain how new businesses sometimes cause the end of old ones. For example, think about cars and horses. The first cars did not disrupt or change peoples' habits around using horses for transportation. Why? The reason is that the first cars were too expensive. Only the wealthiest people could afford one.

Looking for Examples

When you read, look for examples to make sure that ideas are backed up by specific facts or explanations. Examples in a text make the text easier to understand.

Reading 1 uses examples to help you better understand the information in the text. Sometimes, particular phrases are used to introduce examples: *for example* (*e.g.*), *for instance*, *such as*, and *like*. Use the abbreviation *e.g.* when listing examples and *i.e.* (that is) when explaining something in other words.

A. Scan this excerpt from Reading 1. Highlight the words or phrases that introduce examples and explanations. Then underline the examples and explanations.

> Many industries' experiences with disruptive innovation are similar. For example, most homes once had one or more landline phones, connected to the wall by electrical wires. Similar phones were common on street corners. But the new mobile phone prices quickly dropped (i.e., from $3,995 in 1983). Now, many homes do not have landline phones. Instead, each family member has a mobile phone.

B. If there are no good examples, question the ideas in the text. Read the following sentences and write your own example for each one.

1. Many businesses provide things everyone uses, such as *computers, paper, and copy machines.*

2. Education was disrupted, for example, by _____

3. Communication was disrupted by new technologies (e.g., _____)

4. Online services disrupt the way we now share photos, (i.e., _____)

5. Many innovators are disrupting old businesses such as _____

READING ❶   From Horses to Email

Change is often unexpected. The Japanese company Sony changed how people experienced music by introducing a portable music player, the Walkman. In 1979, small radios were extremely popular, but this was the first time you could play the music you wanted while you walked around. Today, people can listen to thousands of songs on their mobile phones. However, small radios are no longer common. How does one technology disrupt another?

In the following exercises, explore key words from Reading 1.

A. Fill in the blanks with the correct words to complete the paragraph.

certain industries popularity production realize term

Over the long _____, many _____ are replaced.

They are often replaced because people _____ something new

is better. For example, _____ kinds of wooden surfboards were

in _____ in Hawaii for hundreds of years. For a time, there was

a large industry involved in making them. But now they don't have the same

_____ because more modern materials, like plastic and

fibreglass, are lighter and stronger than wood.

B. When you learn a new word, learn its different forms. For example, the word *production* is related to *product* (noun), *produce* (present tense verb), *producing* (present progressive), *produced* (past tense), and *will produce* (future tense). Fill in words related to *disappear*.

PLURAL: *disappearances*

NOUN: *disappearance*

RELATED WORD: *appear*

DISAPPEAR (PRESENT TENSE)

FUTURE TENSE:

PAST TENSE:

PRESENT PROGRESSIVE TENSE:

C. What do the words in bold mean to you? Complete the sentences.

1 What is something you know for **certain**?

I know for certain _____

_____

2 What is a type of media that may **disappear**?

A type of media _____

3 Which type of social media is increasing in **popularity**?

_____ is increasing in popularity.

4 What have you **realized** you're good at?

I realized I'm good at _____

5 Do you have a long-**term** plan?

My long-term plan is _____

_____

Before You Read

A. Reading 1 is about the history of disruptive technologies. Read the first paragraph and write a definition of *disruptive innovation*.

_____

_____

B. Write examples of innovations that have or will disrupt old businesses.

OLD GOODS AND SERVICES	DISRUPTIVE INNOVATIONS
1 riding horses	*driving cars*
2 landline phones	*mobile phones*
3 writing letters	
4 human-powered bicycles	
5 electricity from burning coal	

While You Read

C. While you read, look for words or phrases that introduce examples and underline the examples.

From Horses to Email

habits (n.): things you do regularly

wealthiest (adj.): people with the most money

afford (v.): have enough money to pay for

standardized (adj.): make everything the same

assembly lines (n.): workers and machines putting a product together

In 1995, Harvard University's Clayton Christensen was the first to use the **term** *disruptive innovation*. He used the term to explain how new businesses sometimes cause the end of old ones. For example, think about cars and horses. The first cars
5 did not disrupt or change peoples' **habits** around using horses for transportation. Why? The reason is that the first cars were too expensive. Only the **wealthiest** people could **afford** one.

But this changed with Henry Ford's introduction of his Model T cars (1908). His joke was that you could have one in any color that you wanted, as long as it was black.
10 This was part of his secret to success: he **standardized production** and used **assembly lines**. Early cars' hand-made production took a long time for the highly skilled workers.

But Ford produced cars quickly by having each worker's job limited to adding one small part (e.g., one wheel).
15 When Ford's cheap cars became available, the use of horses for daily transportation began to **disappear**.

What will replace cars? Right now, there are already self-driving cars and electric
20 cars. Like the first cars, they are also very expensive. But if prices become cheaper, many people will choose them.

connected (v.): brought together, joined

weatherproof (adj.): avoids bad weather, such as rain

Many **industries'** experiences with disruptive innovation are similar. For example, 25 most homes once had one or more landline phones, **connected** to the wall by electrical wires. Similar phones were common on street corners. But new mobile phone prices quickly dropped (i.e., from $3,995 in 1983). Now, many homes do not have landline phones. Instead, each family member has a mobile phone.

With any disruptive innovation's new technology, there is usually something different 30 and better. The first cars could go faster and were more **weatherproof**. People could use the first mobile phones when they walked down a street or drove a car.

The Internet's introduction of email is a bigger disruption. Before email, people mostly wrote letters, sometimes several each day. The British mathematician, Bertrand Russell (1872–1970), for example, wrote more than 30,000 letters. When email began as a

35 way for a group of university professors to share scientific information, they **realized** it was also a good way to share personal information. Email's **popularity** quickly grew. It was much faster than sending a letter and 40 you could include files with it, such as photos, music, and video. People still write letters, but fewer and fewer.

Now, many innovators look at email and other technologies to find ways to disrupt them. 45 Twitter's 140-character format, for example, meets a need for people to share what they are doing at the moment. Others try to do the same with short video messages.

It's **certain** that disruptive innovations will 50 continue to appear.

(441 words)

After You Read

D. Indicate whether these statements are true or false, according to the text.

STATEMENTS	TRUE	FALSE
❶ Clayton Christensen was probably a professor.		
❷ Cars replaced horses because they had many advantages.		
❸ Model T cars were available in any color you wanted.		
❹ Self-driving and electric cars will never replace today's cars.		
❺ The home landline phone will likely disappear.		
❻ It's still common for people to write thousands of letters.		
❼ Email began as a way to share scientific information.		
❽ Disruptive innovations will probably not continue.		

E. Match the main idea from each paragraph to its example. Scan the text to check your answers.

MAIN IDEAS		EXAMPLES
❶ Mobile phones mean people no longer need older technologies.	_____	a) horses
❷ Cheap cars with new features replace older technologies.	_____	b) Model T cars
❸ Disruptions happen when new products become cheaper.	_____	c) self-driving and electric cars
❹ New features, like being weatherproof, make a new technology attractive.	_____	d) landline phones
❺ Old technologies, like letters, may not disappear but become less important.	_____	e) cars and mobile phones
❻ Even email can be improved upon and replaced.	_____	f) letters and email
❼ Assembly lines help make things cheaper.	_____	g) Twitter

F. Reading 1 suggests that disruptive innovations will continue. Gas-powered cars replaced horses and it seems electric cars will replace gas cars. What's next? Think about electric cars, mobile phones, and text and video messages. Choose one and predict something that might replace one of them. Discuss your ideas with a partner.

FOCUS ON GRAMMAR

Possessive Form

Use the possessive form to make your sentences shorter and clearer.

Examples: The **profits of Amazon** were slow to materialize.
Amazon's profits were slow to materialize.
The **strategic focus of the company** is on growth.
The **company's strategic focus** is on growth.

To show possession, add an apostrophe -s ('s) to singular nouns, if the noun does not already end in -s. For plural nouns, or nouns that end in -s, just add an apostrophe.

Examples: the student**'s** book
the book**'s** pages
the business' address

Never use an apostrophe with possessive pronouns like *his, hers, its, yours, theirs,* or *ours.*

For proper nouns that end in -s, add apostrophe only or an apostrophe -s.

Example: Charles' dog

"It's" is the contraction for "it is."

A. Fill in the blanks with the correct form of the possessive: an apostrophe or an apostrophe -*s*.

1. Sarah_____ friends wanted her to start a new company.

2. They needed her car and asked for her parents_____ garage.

3. The company would collect people_____ unused tools.

4. The company_____ income would come from renting the tools.

5. The tools_____ maintenance would be done by one of the friends.

6. Another friend_____ marketing experience would help promote the company.

B. Rewrite these sentences in the possessive form. Use possessive pronouns where needed.

1. The parents of Sarah weren't so sure.

   Sarah's parents weren't so sure.

2. They wondered where the car they owned would go.

   _____

   _____

3. They asked the parents of the friends what they thought.

   _____

   _____

4. The opinions of the other parents were that it was too much trouble.

   _____

   _____

5. They told Sarah that the garage they owned was not available.

   _____

   _____

6. They said the idea of her friends would not work.

   _____

   _____

Visit My eLab to complete
Grammar Review exercises
for this chapter.

READING ② **Disrupting the Classroom**

All that is necessary for education is a teacher and a student. But since ancient times, classrooms have also featured technology—though that technology continues to evolve: from written records on clay to animal skins to paper and, now, to computer screens. Computers have changed the way students find and use information. What will education look like in a hundred years?

In the following exercises, explore key words from Reading 2.

A. Match each word to its synonym.

WORDS		SYNONYMS
❶ access (n.)	_____	a) benefits
❷ advantages (n.)	_____	b) more and more
❸ development (n.)	_____	c) permission to use
❹ happened (v.)	_____	d) effect
❺ impact (n.)	_____	e) things
❻ increasingly (adv.)	_____	f) growth
❼ materials (n.)	_____	g) occurred

B. Draw an arrow ↓ to indicate where the word in parentheses should be placed in the sentence.

❶ (increasingly) University students today use computer tablets .

❷ (materials) Other cultures started reading and writing with different .

❸ (happened) More mistakes when texts were re-copied .

❹ (access) Girls and women had to new ideas .

❺ (impact) Disruptive technologies' on education continues .

C. What do the words in bold mean to you? Complete the sentences .

❶ To study, what do you need **access** to?

I need access to _____

❷ What's an **advantage** of learning with a computer?

An advantage is _____

_____

❸ What **happened** on the way to class?

On the way to class _____

_____

❹ What is the **impact** of mobile phones on friendships?

The impact of mobile phones is _____

_____

❺ What **materials** do you use when you study?

When I study, I use _____

_____

Before You Read

A. Scan Reading 2 to find these things. Then number them in the order in which they are mentioned.

○ computer tablet

○ illuminated manuscript

○ radio courses

○ clay tablet

○ printed page

B. Will computer tablets replace books? Why or why not? Discuss with a partner.

While You Read

C. While you read, underline examples of learning technologies.

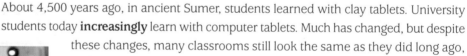

Disrupting the Classroom

immune (adj.): protected from things

About 4,500 years ago, in ancient Sumer, students learned with clay tablets. University students today **increasingly** learn with computer tablets. Much has changed, but despite these changes, many classrooms still look the same as they did long ago, 5 with a teacher standing in the front of the classroom and students sitting in rows. In some ways, education may seem **immune** to disruption. But it's not true: teaching and learning are changing in many ways.

Technology disrupts classrooms, and while clay tablets were popular for thousand years in some places, other cultures started reading and writing 10 with different **materials**. These included dried animal skins used for illuminated manuscripts. These manuscripts' colourful handwritten and illustrated pages were copied one page at a time. But the people who copied them often made mistakes. More mistakes **happened** when texts were re-copied. It's an example of each new technology's problems as 15 well as **advantages**.

Europeans' **development** of printing presses and paper books began in the mid-1400s. Printing presses' accuracy and speed overcame the disadvantages of hand-copied books. Postman (1993) writes,

winepress (n.): machine to get juice from grapes

moveable type (n.): letters on individual blocks used in printing

previously (adv.): at an earlier time

correspondence courses (n.): lessons sent by mail

collection (n.): group of things

20 Forty years after Gutenberg converted an old **winepress** into a printing machine with **moveable type**, there were presses in 110 cities in six countries. Fifty years after the press was invented, more than eight million books had been printed, almost all of them filled with information that had **previously** been unavailable to the average person. (p. 61)

This meant more people, especially girls and women, had **access** to new ideas and 25 they could educate themselves.

Disruptive technologies' **impact** on education continues. In 1840, the new British postal service led to the development of **correspondence courses**. By 1938, hundreds of universities used radio to teach courses. In 1953, a university in Texas offered TV's first university course. And, in 1989, the University of Phoenix's Bachelor's and 30 Master's degree courses started online, using the Internet.

This last technology, the Internet, is causing education's greatest disruptions. With the Internet, more people can learn more things than ever before. Students' access to materials is now much greater than the one or two textbooks usually used in a course. The Internet offers much more information than a university library's 35 **collection** of materials.

The Internet's biggest disruption of learning is about students' participation. Students no longer want to simply sit and listen to a lecture. They want to be involved in their own learning. They want to discuss ideas. Online learning makes that possible with chat lines during lectures and discussion forums after. In discussion forums, students 40 share ideas in text and images. For example, they can post a photo or a graph that supports an argument. Even during traditional lectures, students' Twitter messages comment on what the lecturer is saying.

What will be the next disruption to education? (461 words)

Six hundred years before, Gutenberg, Chinese, and then Koreans and Japanese, used wood blocks to print whole pages.

Reference

Postman, N. (1993). *Technopoly: The surrender of culture to technology*. Toronto: Random House.

After You Read

D. Scan the paragraphs to understand the main points in the table. Then, write an impact or an example for each point.

MAIN POINTS	EXAMPLES
❶ many classrooms look the same	*teacher in front/students in rows*
❷ reading and writing with different materials	
❸ printing presses	*accuracy and speed*
❹ eight million books printed	
❺ new British postal service	*correspondence courses*
❻ radio, TV and Internet	
❼ Internet	*more information than a university library*
❽ students' participation	
❾ students share ideas	

E. Choose the word in parentheses that best completes each sentence.

1 The use of clay tablets and computer tablets makes it seem education has not (changed / disappeared).

2 Illuminated manuscripts were beautiful but the process of making them led to many (mistakes / copies).

3 The widespread use of the printing press suggests people were (uninterested / interested) in learning.

4 Radio courses are probably no longer popular because TV and computers have other (advantages / disadvantages).

5 The Internet is a bigger educational disruption because it offers (more / less) access to learning materials.

6 Students now want to be more (online / involved) during university lectures.

FOCUS ON WRITING

Writing Simple Messages

You write simple messages on paper and online for different purposes. You may want to ask for help, for more information, for permission, or to apologize, thank, or congratulate someone. Messages can be formal or informal, but both have things in common. Here are some rules to follow.

• Plan what you want to write. Make your message simple and easy to understand.

• Know the person you are writing to. Make sure you are writing to the right person. Consider how formal you should be.

• In formal emails, include reasons along with examples or explanations as necessary. It should be clear why you are writing.

• In formal emails, include a proper greeting and a friendly goodbye.

A. Draw arrows to connect the notes in blue to the parts of the message each refers to.

Include a date, if not done ⟶ January 15
automatically.

State the reason for writing, in this case, a problem.

Include your request, in this case, to ask for more time.

If necessary, include an action such as a request for a reply.

> January 15
>
> John,
> I can't finish my part of this week's assignment by Friday. Can we write Ms. Green and ask for more time? I'm sure I could finish it by Monday morning.
>
> Let me know.
> Jenny

> When you write a message, remember to check your spelling and grammar!

B. What is the purpose of the message in task A? Choose the best ones.

☐ ask for help   ☐ apologize to someone
☐ ask for more information ☐ thank someone
☐ ask for permission   ☐ congratulate someone

WARM-UP ASSIGNMENT
Write an Informal Message

In Focus on Writing, you learned about writing messages for different purposes. In this Warm-Up Assignment, you will write an informal message to a partner to share a famous business person's achievements.

A. Decide which business person you will write about. Try to find one who has disrupted an industry, such as someone who has founded a start-up.

B. Plan what you want to write. Give the name and a one-sentence explanation of who the business person is. Use the possessive form to describe the person's achievements.

C. Write your message. Make it simple and easy to understand. Use the informal message format in Focus on Writing.

D. Check your message.
- ☐ Are all the words spelled correctly?
- ☐ Is your grammar correct?
- ☐ Did you use the correct punctuation?
- ☐ Did you use the possessive form?

E. Read your message aloud. Are there any other errors? Make corrections and write your final copy.

F. Share your message with your partner.

Use feedback from your teacher and classmates on this Warm-Up Assignment to improve your writing.

READING ❸ — Learning from Short-Term Setbacks

At some point in your life you have faced difficulties and obstacles to success. How did you react? Some people are upset by challenges and decide to do something else. Other people might enjoy a challenge and keep working until they achieve their objective. In the same way, every business has times when progress seems impossible and difficult decisions need to be made.

VOCABULARY BUILD

In the following exercises, explore key words from Reading 3.

A. Scan Reading 3 for these words. Look at the context (the surrounding words) to help you understand the meaning. Write a definition for each word. For words you are not sure of, use a dictionary.

1. appreciate: *recognize*
2. criticized: *pointed out*
3. perspective: *point of view for*
4. potential: *possibility of*
5. revenue: *income of*

B. Collocations are words typically used together. For example, the words *salt* and *pepper* are often used together and in that order. Look at these words and indicate whether each one usually goes with *investment*, *consumer*, or both. The words may come before or after *consumer* or *investment*.

WORDS	consumer	investment	BOTH
1 energy			
2 foreign			
3 rights			
4 safe			
5 short-term			
6 spending			

C. The word *consumer* is a role in society. Look at three related roles and give a definition for each one.

1 producer: _____

2 user: _____

3 seller: _____

D. What do the words in bold mean to you? Complete the sentences.

1 How are you different from other **consumers**?

I'm different from other consumers because _____

_____

2 What is something you **appreciate**?

Something I appreciate is _____

_____

3 What is something you might **criticize**?

I might criticize _____

_____

4 What kind of **investments** would you like to make?

I would like to make _____

_____

5 What is your **perspective** on starting a business?

My perspective on starting a business is _____

_____

Before You Read

A. Reading 3 notes that, "One myth about rich people is that they always succeed." What is your opinion about the qualities or personalities of rich people? Indicate what you believe.

RICH PEOPLE ARE ...	MYTH	TRUE
❶ competitive		
❷ creative		
❸ greedy		
❹ impatient		
❺ lazy		
❻ organized		

B. Reading 3 is about Jeff Bezos and Amazon, the company he started. Write three things you know about Bezos or Amazon.

❶ _____

❷ _____

❸ _____

While You Read

C. Many entrepreneurs face setbacks (problems). While you read, underline the setbacks faced by Amazon and its founder, Jeff Bezos.

Learning from Short-Term Setbacks

adversity (n.): difficulty or misfortune

setbacks (n.): reverse in progress

One lesson that stands out among those offered by the careers of many billionaires is the importance of overcoming **adversity** and learning from short-term ups and downs. One myth about rich people is that they always succeed. In fact, many
5 entrepreneurs suffered early, even repeated, **setbacks** but demonstrated resilience and went on to achieve long-term success by learning from their failures. Patience and the ability to keep a lengthy time horizon in view are key qualities that distinguish the ultra wealthy from many other people.

10 Early in his career, for example, Jeff Bezos experienced business difficulties. He had the novel idea that the Internet could serve as a platform for a successful retail operation, and in 1994, he founded Amazon as an online bookseller. Even though people were
15 used to walking into stores and physically touching products, Bezos thought that **consumers** would like the convenience of online shopping and **appreciate** being able to compare different products while at home.

allure (n.): attraction

prognosticators (n.): people who predict the future

persistence (n.): determination to work at something

pan out (v.): work in the end

20 Despite the seeming **allure** of that idea, Amazon's profits were slow to materialize. For years, investors questioned his quarterly results while critics doubted his business model and claimed that he was failing as a businessman. Some argued that the company would never make money and **criticized** Bezos for spending too much on digital infrastructure. The negative commentary continued into the 2000s, when the
25 company moved into cloud computing with Amazon Web Services and Kindle book readers. Outside observers questioned each decision on the grounds that it distracted from the company's strategic focus and would require expensive **investments**. Some **prognosticators** forecast permanent damage to the company.

Yet Bezos stayed focused on the long term, and his **persistence** paid off. Soon Amazon
30 was earning more than $50 billion in **revenue** and had solidified its place as the dominant online retailer for a wide range of products. No longer was the company limited to books. Instead, consumers could purchase thousands of different items, and businesses could lease space on the Amazon cloud. Amazon became a leader in retailing and providing real-time business analytics for a number of different corporations.

35 Bezos explained his approach as follows: "We don't give up on things easily. Our third-party seller business is an example of that. It took us three tries to get the third-party seller business to work. We didn't give up. If you're not stubborn, you'll give up on experiments too soon," he said. In his opinion, persistence was the key to his business success. Too many leaders have a short-term **perspective** that blinds them to long-term
40 opportunities. Investing money and demanding a quick return is not the way to build a successful company—it often takes years for investments to **pan out**. Patience is a major virtue, especially in industries with strong long-term growth **potential**.

Later, he added, "There's no lone genius who figures it all out and sends down the magic formula (for success). You study, you debate, you brainstorm, and the answers
45 start to emerge. It takes time. Nothing happens quickly in this mode."   (495 words)

West, D.M. (2014). *Billionaires: Reflections on the upper crust* (pp. 142–144). Washington: The Brookings Institute Press.

After You Read

D. Choose the word or phrase that best completes each sentence, according to the text.

1 In short-term ups and downs, the downs refer to _____.

    a) opportunities   b) innovations   c) challenges

2 Repeated setbacks means a company usually needs to _____.

    a) start over   b) open   c) ignore workers

3 An Internet retail platform was disruptive because it did not require _____.

    a) cash payments   b) any employees   c) physical stores

4 Because profits were slow to materialize, investors were _____.

    a) happy   b) worried   c) encouraged

5 To be the dominant player in the market means Amazon is the _____.

    a) least popular   b) most popular   c) most copied

E. Give examples to support either the *yes* answer or the *no* answer. Scan Reading 3 if you need help. Discuss your examples with a partner.

1 Jeff Bezos was successful at other jobs.

☐ Yes, for example, *he was already successful in banking.* _____

☐ No, for example, _____

2 Successful business people are sometimes simply lucky.

☐ Yes, for example, _____

_____

☐ No, for example, _____

_____

3 Bezos's critics probably feel they were correct.

☐ Yes, for example, _____

_____

☐ No, for example, _____

_____

4 Amazon's early lack of profits was not a problem.

☐ Yes, for example, _____

_____

☐ No, for example, _____

_____

Academic
Survival Skill

Boosting Your Vocabulary

Could you see more colours if you knew more colour words? The answer is yes. Vocabulary helps you experience, understand, and remember the world better. Vocabulary helps you name more things and actions. There are many ways to expand your vocabulary, but just finding new words is not enough. You need to be able to remember their meaning and how they are spelled and pronounced.

Keep a list of new words: words you hear and words you read. When you write a new word, check its spelling and write its definition. The easiest way to define a word is by using a synonym. But before you do, consider how the two words might differ.

A. The words *appreciate* and *like* are synonyms, but they are slightly different. Indicate whether each definition in the table is for *appreciate* or for *like* or for both. If you are not sure, use a dictionary.

DEFINITIONS		*appreciate*	*like*	BOTH
❶	approve			
❷	grateful for (something)			
❸	recognize what something is worth			
❹	find enjoyable			
❺	rise in value or price			
❻	understand (a situation)			

B. Another way to learn new vocabulary is to draw a mind map that shows how words relate. Look at this mind map for the word *disruption*. Which words can you add to those already there?

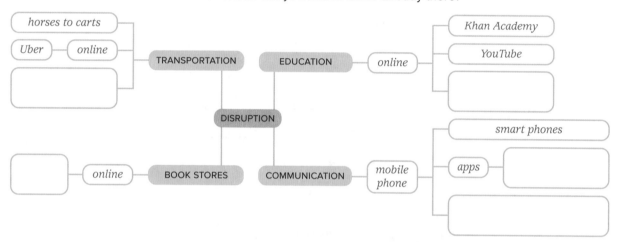

C. A third way to learn new vocabulary is to identify words in context. Read this excerpt from Reading 3. Then write the part of speech and the meaning of the words in bold. If you are not sure, use a dictionary.

> In fact, many **entrepreneurs** suffered early, even repeated, setbacks but demonstrated **resilience** and went on to achieve long-term success by learning from their failures. Patience and the ability to keep a lengthy time **horizon** in view are key qualities that **distinguish** the **ultra** wealthy from many other people.

❶ entrepreneurs: *(noun) business people who start something new* _____

❷ resilience: _____

❸ horizon: _____

❹ distinguish: _____

❺ ultra: _____

❗ Words like "ultra" are often combined with other words to give them a new meaning.

FINAL ASSIGNMENT

Write a Formal Email

Use what you learned in this chapter to write a formal email to your teacher. You are going to do a project on the business person you chose in the Warm-Up Assignment. Ask your teacher to approve your choice.

A. Use your message from the Warm-Up Assignment (page 75) to write a draft of your email. Build on what you learned in Focus on Writing (page 74).

- In the *To* line, write your teacher's email address.
- In the *Subject* line, briefly explain why you are writing: for example, Business person for English 101, Assignment 1.
- In the body of the email, include a proper greeting: *Dear _____*. Use *Ms.*, *Mrs.*, *Mr.*, or *Dr.*, and the teacher's last name followed with a comma.
- Explain why you are interested in this person and give an example of his or her achievements. Use the possessive form (see Focus on Grammar, page 69).
- Conclude by asking that your choice be approved. Offer to answer additional questions if necessary.
- End with *Yours sincerely*, or *Sincerely*, include your first and last name and something else to identify you, such as your student number.

B. Refer to the Models Chapter (page 166) to see an example of a formal email and to learn more about how to write one.

C. Proofread your email message. Use the checklist from the Warm-Up Assignment.

D. Read your email aloud. Are there any other errors? Make corrections and write a final copy.

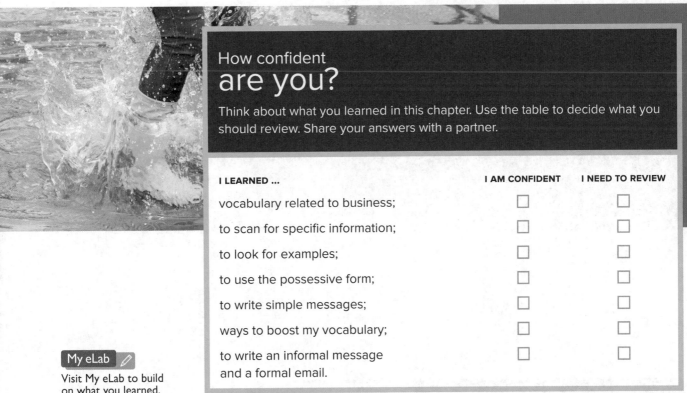

How confident are you?

Think about what you learned in this chapter. Use the table to decide what you should review. Share your answers with a partner.

I LEARNED ...	I AM CONFIDENT	I NEED TO REVIEW
vocabulary related to business;	☐	☐
to scan for specific information;	☐	☐
to look for examples;	☐	☐
to use the possessive form;	☐	☐
to write simple messages;	☐	☐
ways to boost my vocabulary;	☐	☐
to write an informal message and a formal email.	☐	☐

My eLab

Visit My eLab to build on what you learned.

CHAPTER 5

A Personal World

The steam engine was invented in 1781. It was used to power industrial machines, ships, and trains. People did not expect to have steam engines in their homes. But today, countless new industrial technologies, from lasers to drones, have home applications. Many smaller, cheaper, and faster computer-based technologies are necessary parts of everyday life. Which modern technologies are most important in your life?

In this chapter,
you will

- learn vocabulary related to personal technology;

- recognize comparisons in texts;

- analyze information in charts;

- review the future tense with *will* and *be going to*;

- learn block and point-by-point methods of comparison;

- learn ways to work with others;

- create a Venn diagram and write a comparison paragraph.

GEARING UP

A. Look at the diagram and then answer the questions.

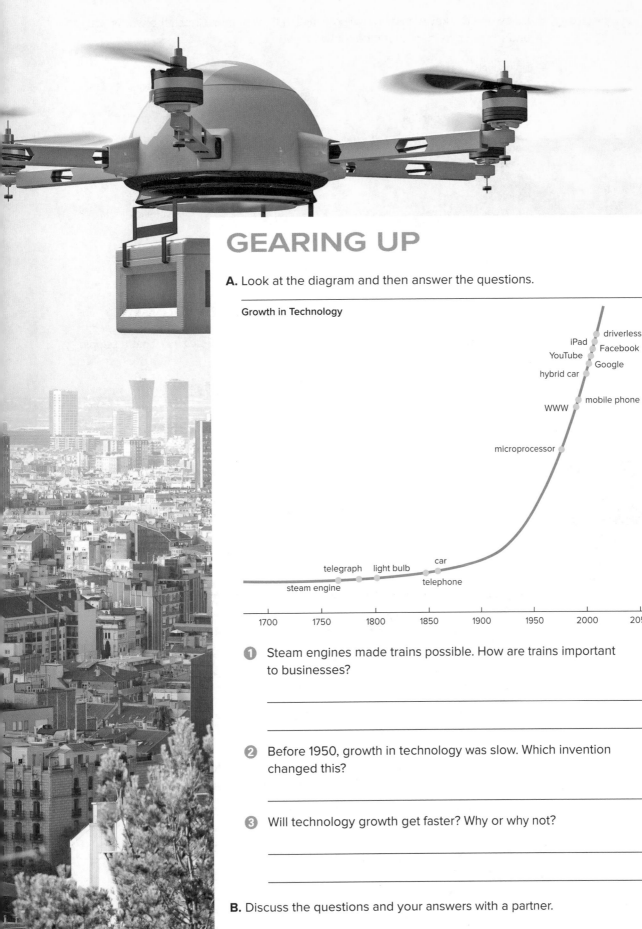

Growth in Technology

1. Steam engines made trains possible. How are trains important to businesses?

   _____

   _____

2. Before 1950, growth in technology was slow. Which invention changed this?

   _____

3. Will technology growth get faster? Why or why not?

   _____

   _____

B. Discuss the questions and your answers with a partner.

Below are the key words you will practise in this chapter. Check the words you understand and then underline the words you use.

nouns
budget
campaigns
crisis
expenses
options
progress
versions

adjectives
particular
personal
private
virtual

personal technology

verbs
depends
experience
imagine
improve
maintain
measure
prepare
satisfy
spread
survive

These words are from the Longman Communication 3000 and the Academic Word List. See Appendix 1, page 172.

FOCUS ON READING

Recognizing Comparisons in Texts

When you read, look for comparisons. Comparisons show how two or more people, places, or things are similar.

Example: The invention of the steam engine is similar to the invention of the Internet.

Comparisons often use words or phrases such as *both*, *too*, *as well as*, *in the same way*.

You can also compare people, places, or things using the comparative or superlative form of an adjective or an adverb.

Comparative adjectives are used to compare two people, places, or things. Superlative adjectives are used to compare three or more people, places, or things. Form the comparative by adding *-er* to the end of the adjective. Form the superlative by adding *-est* to the end of the adjective.

ADJECTIVE	COMPARATIVE FORM	SUPERLATIVE FORM
cheap	cheaper	cheapest
smart	smarter	smartest

Some adjectives follow different rules or have irregular comparative and superlative forms.

Examples: popular → more popular → the most popular
good ⟶ better ⟶ best

Underline the comparative and superlative forms in the following sentences. Then write whether each is comparative (C) or superlative (S).

1 Imagine you are the <u>worst</u> off among them, without electricity for two years.   *S*

2 It will be quieter than you can remember, with no cars, radios, or TVs.   _____

3 The food in your fridge will be the quickest to rot. _____

4 The most serious crisis will start at a nuclear power plant. _____

5 Life in the countryside will be easier than life in the city. _____

6 The best chance to survive will be to find a farm. _____

Analyzing Information in Charts

Sometimes information is presented visually, in diagrams, graphs, and charts. Charts summarize numbers and ideas. This makes the information easier to understand. When you look at different types of charts, consider how the information is organized.

A. Look at these three charts. Read the kind of information each one presents.

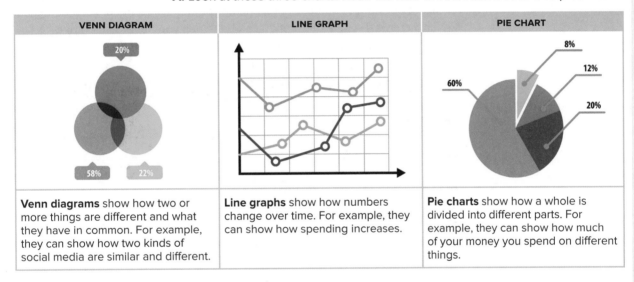

VENN DIAGRAM	LINE GRAPH	PIE CHART
Venn diagrams show how two or more things are different and what they have in common. For example, they can show how two kinds of social media are similar and different.	**Line graphs** show how numbers change over time. For example, they can show how spending increases.	**Pie charts** show how a whole is divided into different parts. For example, they can show how much of your money you spend on different things.

B. Match the information to the correct chart.

INFORMATION		CHARTS
1 a comparison of the features of two computers	_____	a) line graph
2 average time spent in a day on seven activities	_____	b) pie chart
3 changing ages for kids having their first phones	_____	c) Venn diagram

READING ❶   Smaller, Faster, Cheaper

In an 1899 cartoon, a boy says, "Everything that can be invented has been invented." The statement was not true then and is even less true now. New inventions are introduced every day. This is partly because there are new materials and new ways to make things. It is also because the market for small inventions is so great. What new invention would you like to have?

In the following exercises, explore key words from Reading 1.

A. Choose the best synonym for each word in bold.

1 They worked hard to **improve** the computer system.

    a) develop   b) reject   c) maintain

2 He was **particular** about where to study.

    a) specific   b) strange   c) unusual

3 There were many **versions** of the song online.

    a) costs   b) copies   c) fans

4 She made **progress** on her homework last night.

    a) notes   b) an advance   c) complaints

B. The words *personal* and *private* can be synonyms. They both refer to things you might not want to share. But sometimes personal information can be things like family news. Private information can be things you never want others to know, like computer passwords. Look at the following examples and indicate whether you think each one is *personal*, *private,* or both.

EXAMPLES	*personal*	*private*	BOTH
1 stories about when you were young			
2 your friend's special name for you			
3 who you like			
4 financial information			
5 future plans			
6 your grades			

C. What do the words in bold mean to you? Complete the sentences.

1 Which **particular** technology do you use every day?

Every day I use _____

2 What is one way you **measure** success?

I measure success _____

3 What's a **personal** thing you're proud of?

I'm proud of _____

_____

4 What sort of information doesn't need to be **private**?

Information that doesn't need to be private is _____

_____

Before You Read

A. Look at this line chart. It shows the growth of personal electronic devices. Then answer the questions.

Predicted Use of Internet Devices

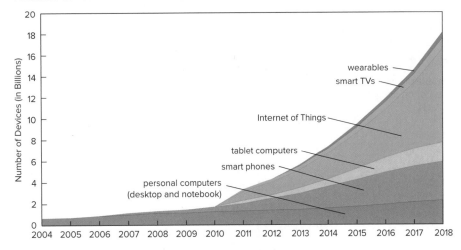

1. Which type of device is growing in use the most?

    a) wearables
    b) tablet computers
    c) smart phones

2. Which of the following reaches two billion devices in 2018?

    a) smart phones
    b) Internet of Things
    c) personal computers

3. After wearables, what are the most popular devices?

    a) smart phones
    b) smart TVs
    c) Internet of Things

B. Write one question you have about the Internet of Things. Use *who, what, when, where, why,* or *how.* Discuss your question with a partner.

While You Read

C. While you read, underline comparative and superlative words and phrases. This will help you answer questions in task E.

Smaller, Faster, Cheaper

> Megabytes, gigabytes, and terabytes are measures of data. Each one is 1,024 times larger than the one before it.

We can now easily predict the future. We are no longer surprised when things are smaller, faster, and cheaper. One example is computer data. The first hard drives were the size of refrigerators. Despite this, they
5 could only store about 5 megabytes of data and cost thousands of dollars. In comparison, the cheapest 128-gigabyte USB stick can store 25,600 times that amount. Modern computers process large amounts of data
10 almost instantly.

What will the future look like with smaller, faster, and cheaper technologies? As well as cheaper data, other computer parts will be cheap and used in different devices.

15 In **particular**, devices in our homes will include small computer processors. **Sensors** will **measure** everything from temperature to noise. This leads to the Internet of Things (IOT). The IOT will let your **appliances** talk to each other through wireless network connections. For example, when your computer printer senses that ink supplies are low, it will **automatically** add *inks* to your phone's shopping list.

20 In the same way, companies are suddenly adding technology to the most popular tools such as vacuum cleaners. A company called iRobot introduced the Roomba vacuum cleaner in 2002. It is easier than pushing it around like other vacuum cleaners. When you **install** it in your home, it will follow a program to wander around and vacuum your floors on its own. The best thing is that when it starts to lose power, it 25 will go to a wall socket and charge itself. Other **versions** will wash your floors.

How will the IOT **improve** this? The appliance company Dyson is going to introduce a similar robotic vacuum cleaner. But it will connect to a phone app to show your vacuum's **progress** on a map of your home. You will also control the vacuum cleaner from your phone.

30 In the future, you will watch your home from video cameras in different rooms. You will use other sensors to **track** what is going on. For example, a noise sensor will give you the quickest warning when your dog barks. Is there is a thief outside the door? Is your dog scared of your vacuum cleaner? Is your dog hungry? When your dog is hungry, how are you going to feed it? Perhaps you will have a smarter choice: a phone-35 controlled dog feeder.

Compared to 2010, when there were few connected devices on the IOT, by 2018, there will be 18 billion. These will include computers, tablets, phones, and TVs, as well as **wearables**. These wearables, like fitness trackers and **personal** clip-on cameras, are going to share your information like your location with other devices. If you are 40 almost home, sensors will check the refrigerator to make sure you have food. Other devices will adjust the temperature and start your favourite music. For many people, the IOT will be like a team of **private** servants, each thinking how to best serve your needs.

(482 words)

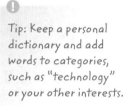

Tip: Keep a personal dictionary and add words to categories, such as "technology" or your other interests.

After You Read

D. Connect the phrases to summarize Reading 1.

SUMMARY		
❶ Data and other computer parts ...	_____	a) a robotic vacuum cleaner.
❷ The IOT will let your appliances talk to each other ...	_____	b) to your devices.
❸ iRobot introduced the Roomba, ...	_____	c) through wireless connections.
❹ Sensors will tell you what ...	_____	d) take care of you like servants.
❺ Wearables will give information about you ...	_____	e) will be cheaper.
❻ Your devices will ...	_____	f) happens in your home.

E. Review the comparative and superlative words and phrases you underlined in Reading 1. Then indicate whether these statements are true or false, according to the text.

STATEMENTS	TRUE	FALSE
1 The cheapest 128-gigabyte USB stick can store much less than the first hard drives.		
2 Data will be cheaper and computer parts will be expensive.		
3 Using a Roomba is easier than pushing around other vacuum cleaners.		
4 The best thing is that robot vacuum cleaners will charge themselves.		
5 A noise sensor won't give you the quickest warning.		
6 A smarter choice will be a phone-controlled dog feeder.		

FOCUS ON GRAMMAR

The contracted form of "will not" is "won't."

My eLab

Visit My eLab to complete Grammar Review exercises for this chapter.

Future Tense with *Will* and *Be Going To*

In Reading 1, you read predictions about future technologies. When you write about the future, you use the future tense: *will* and *be going to*. You also use the future tense when you want to talk or write about plans or promises. Here are some simple rules for using either form.

• Use *will* in front of the base form of the main verb.

  Examples: What **will** happen to those people?
            You **will** miss your personal technology.

• Use *be going to* in front of the base form of the main verb. Remember to conjugate the verb *be*.

  Examples: What **is going to** happen to those people?
            You **are going to** miss your personal technology.

A. Fill in the blanks with the correct form of the verb in parentheses. Use *will* to form the future tense.

1 It (is) _____ quiet with no cars.

2 You (think) _____ quickly to find enough food.

3 Many people (experience) _____ difficulties.

4 Only bicycle transportation (work) _____.

B. Fill in the blanks with the correct form of the verb in parentheses. Use *be going to* to form the future tense.

1 Who (put) _____ out the fires?

2 You (watch) _____ your home from video cameras.

3 The food in your fridge (rot) _____.

4 Clip-on cameras (share) _____ information about you.

READING ❷ | After the Storm

In 1989, a storm on the surface of the sun exploded outwards. It sent electric and magnetic waves toward Earth. When the waves hit Earth, they caused an electrical blackout in Quebec for nine hours. What would you miss if the power went out for nine hours?

VOCABULARY
BUILD

In the following exercises, explore key words from Reading 2.

A. Choose the best definition for each word. For words you are not sure of, look at the context of the word in Reading 2 for clues. Use a dictionary to check your answers.

1 depends   a) relies on someone or something   b) destroys something

2 experience   a) get rid of something   b) encounter something

3 imagine   a) forget an idea   b) form an idea

4 spread   a) extend over a large area   b) get smaller over time

B. The words *prepare, crisis,* and *survive* can refer to a disaster. Fill in the blanks to complete the paragraph. Use each word three times.

Imagine you are going to _____ for an earthquake. Will you _____ or not? It depends on how much of a _____ it is. A small earthquake is only going to shake your home a little. You don't have to _____. How you _____ a large earthquake will be a bigger _____. Let's say your home falls down. How will you _____ until you find another place to live? If you _____ early, you can have food, water, and a tent ready. But make sure you have more than you need. In a bigger _____, you will want to be able to help others.

C. What do the words in bold mean to you? Complete the sentences.

1 What is one thing you **imagine** about the future?

I imagine _____

_____

2 What is the easiest way to **spread** news?

The easiest way to spread news _____

_____

3 What's the best way to **survive** your first day at college?

The best way to survive _____

_____

4 Who is someone you **depend** on?

Someone I depend on _____

5 What would you like to **experience**?

I'd like to experience _____

_____

Before You Read

A. Power outages (failures) are common. Between 2003 and 2012 in the USA, there were 679 big ones that each affected more than 50,000 people. These power outages cost between $18 and $70 billion a year. Look at this line chart and then answer the questions.

Electric Outages in the USA, 1992–2012

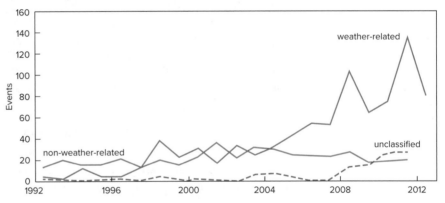

1 What type of outage has recently increased?

a) weather-related causes

b) non-weather related causes

c) unclassified causes

2 Guess the reason why non-weather-related outages have not increased over time.

a) Accident rates stay the same.

b) Accidents are not reported.

c) Few people cause outages.

3 Weather-related outages are often caused by winds breaking electric lines. Why are these outages so expensive?

a) Most people take a day off when it snows.

b) Businesses that depend on electricity lose money.

c) Home owners have to pay for other fuels.

4 Why do you think weather-related outages increased from 1992 to 2012?

a) The weather is worse than it used to be.

b) People are using more electricity.

c) Electrical systems are old and weak.

d) All of the above.

5 What might unclassified outages include?

    a) outages caused by wild animals

    b) outages from unknown causes

    c) outages from electrical failures

While You Read

B. While you read, underline the comparative and superlative words and phrases.

After the Storm

solar (adj.): related to the sun

telegraph (n.): system for sending messages along electric wires

interrupted (v.): stopped temporarily

disruptions (n.): breaks in the way things work

climate (n.): long-term weather

In 1859, a huge storm on the surface of the sun—a **solar** storm—affected Earth's electrical systems. For example, **telegraph** services were **interrupted** and some caught fire. Such storms occur, on average, every 150 years.
5 Another one will probably happen soon.

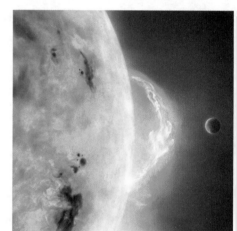

Today, the threat is worse because we rely far more on electricity. Rothkopf (2014) writes, "In the US alone, 130 million people could lose power. As many as forty million Americans
10 could be left with long-term power **disruptions**—anywhere from sixteen days to two years" (para. 5).

What is going to happen to those people? **Imagine** you are the worst off among them,
15 without electricity for two years.

You are going to wake up in the morning without your personal technology. The lights will be off too. It will be quieter than you can remember, with no cars, radios, or TVs. Maybe you live in an apartment. In your kitchen, you will find there is no water because electrical pumps no longer lift water to your floor. The food in your fridge
20 will be the quickest to rot. You will have to cook any meat to save it. But neither your electric stove nor your microwave oven work. Perhaps you can use a barbeque. In cities, there won't be enough food for everyone.

Many people will **experience** difficulties. Only bicycle transportation will work. In hospitals, elevators will stop, and countless medical tools will not work. Medicines
25 that need to be kept cold will be useless.

Fires will start but, without fire trucks, who is going to put them out? These fires will **spread**. The most serious **crisis** will start at a nuclear power plant. Without electricity to pump cold water to cool the reactors, they will overheat and explode, spreading radiation. In 2011, this happened in Fukushima, Japan.

30 To **survive**, you are going to have to go to the countryside.

Compared to life in the city, life in the countryside will be easier. Your best chance to survive will be to find a farm with a variety of plants and animals. But this **depends** on the place, and on the time of year. A solar storm in the middle of a cold winter would be a greater crisis. Few plants will be available and you won't be able to get
35 food for animals such as cows, sheep, and chickens. In a cold **climate**, chickens are not going to survive without warmer buildings to live in.

shelter (n.): a protected place to live, such as your home

It's possible you are going to have to make your own food, clothing, and **shelter**. You will have to take care of yourself when you get sick or if you have an accident. You will need to learn the most common skills people had 150 years ago—but you won't
40 be able to look up those skills on the Internet. Even after the electricity comes back on, it will still take years for life to get back to normal.

Perhaps you should start to **prepare** now.

(493 words)

References

Odenwald, S. (2015, July 31). The day the sun brought darkness. NASA. Retrieved from http://www.nasa.gov/topics/earth/features/sun_darkness.html

Rothkopf, J. (2014, July 29). Billionaire's dire warning: Solar flares could ruin everything. Salon. Retrieved from http://www.salon.com/2014/07/29/billionaire_paul_singer_is_afraid_of_solar_flares_should_we_be_too/

After You Read

C. Match the comparative and superlative words or phrases to the issue each relates to, according to the text.

COMPARATIVE OR SUPERLATIVE		ISSUE EACH RELATES TO
❶ easier	_____	a) the skills people had 150 years ago
❷ greater	_____	b) solar storm threat
❸ most common	_____	c) a world with no cars, radios, or TVs
❹ most serious	_____	d) the crisis from a solar storm in winter
❺ quieter	_____	e) the buildings that chickens need to live in
❻ warmer	_____	f) life in the countryside
❼ worse	_____	g) nuclear power plant explosion

D. Based on your understanding of Reading 2, answer these questions *yes* or *no*. Discuss your answers with a partner.

DURING A TWO-YEAR BLACKOUT, IT WILL BE EASY FOR PEOPLE TO ...	YES	NO
❶ find food.		
❷ stay in the city.		
❸ grow food.		
❹ get transportation.		
❺ live in the countryside.		
❻ learn common skills.		
❼ raise animals for food.		

Comparing in a Paragraph

A comparison paragraph shows similarities between people, places, things, or ideas. Begin your comparison paragraph with a topic sentence. This lets your readers know what you will be comparing.

Example: Watches and wearable fitness trackers are similar in some ways.

After your topic sentence, there are two different ways to write a comparison paragraph.

• The first is the *block method*. In the block method, you write everything about the first thing being compared, then everything about the second thing. When you compare a watch to a fitness tracker, describe all the points of a watch and then all the similar points of a fitness tracker.

Example: You wear a watch on your wrist and it tells the time. Similarly, you wear a fitness tracker on your wrist and it also tells the time.

• The second is the *point-by-point method*. In the point-by-point method, you write each similarity together.

Example: You wear both a watch and a fitness tracker on your wrist. Another similarity is they both tell the time.

Write a conclusion. Say something new about the two things you are comparing. For example, how they might be more or less similar in the future.

Example: Some fitness trackers and some watches have a similar look. In future, fitness trackers and watches will look more like mobile phones.

A. Choose the best topic sentence for a comparison paragraph.

☐ Microwave ovens and refrigerators are both devices.

☐ Microwave ovens and refrigerators can both be connected wirelessly.

☐ Microwave ovens are similar to refrigerators and other devices.

B. Read the paragraphs and write which method of comparison each uses.

PARAGRAPH 1	PARAGRAPH 2
Refrigerators are kitchen appliances that need electricity to work. They cool food and store it until you need it. Similarly, microwave ovens are electric kitchen appliances. They heat food when you need it.	Refrigerators and microwave ovens are both important kitchen appliances and both need electricity. Refrigerators, as well as microwave ovens, are used to prepare food. Refrigerators store food until you need it and microwave ovens cook the food when you need it.
METHOD: _____	METHOD: _____

WARM-UP ASSIGNMENT
Create a Venn Diagram

When you need to compare things, a Venn diagram can help you organize the information (see Focus on Critical Thinking, page 85). This Venn diagram compares life during a long-term power outage. The blue circle shows things you do now. The red circle shows things you might have to do after an outage. The section that overlaps shows things you would continue to do, things that would not change.

Before and After a Long-Term Power Outage

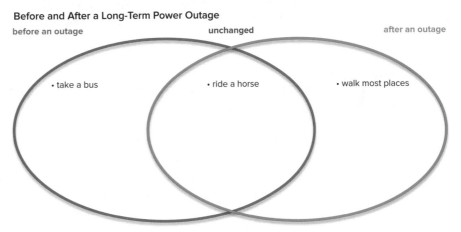

before an outage | unchanged | after an outage

• take a bus | • ride a horse | • walk most places

> ❗ Venn diagrams can compare multiple things. Just add more circles.

A. Based on Reading 2, where in the Venn diagram would you put these activities?

ACTIVITIES	BEFORE AN OUTAGE	UNCHANGED	AFTER AN OUTAGE
❶ use a refrigerator	✓		
❷ make your own clothing			
❸ ride a bicycle			
❹ use a microwave oven			
❺ learn skills from other people			
❻ grow your own food			

B. Write three more activities on the Venn diagram: one thing you do now, one thing that would be unchanged and one thing that would be different.

C. Write two sentences that compare life before and after the outage. Use *will* or *be going to* and the comparative form.

Example: It's easy to ride a bicycle and it **is going to** be **easier** after an outage when there are no cars.

❶ _____

_____

❷ _____

_____

D. Write a sentence to describe one thing that will happen after the outage. Use the future tense and the superlative form: words or phrases such as *best, worst, hardest, easiest, most fun,* or *least fun.*

Example: The **worst** thing after an outage **will** be no electric lights.

_____

_____

E. Proofread your sentences in tasks C and D. Check your spelling and grammar. Make corrections and then share them with a partner.

READING ③

Three Ways Technology Has Changed our Lives for the Better

It's hard to imagine life without technology. Many personal technologies, like electric toothbrushes, are not only more convenient, they are also more effective. Technologies can save you time and make your life easier. One of the biggest uses of personal technology is how you can connect with friends. But some people spend more time with their technologies than they do with their friends.

VOCABULARY BUILD

In the following exercises, explore key words from Reading 3.

A. Match each word to its definition.

WORDS		DEFINITIONS
❶ campaigns	_____	a) keep something at the same level
❷ maintain	_____	b) meet expectations
❸ options	_____	c) not physically existing
❹ satisfy	_____	d) possible choices
❺ virtual	_____	e) sets of actions to reach a goal

B. Three words related to money are *budget, earnings,* and *expenses.* Choose the word in parentheses that best completes the sentence.

❶ He (budgets / expenses) how much he should spend on different things.

❷ Your (expenses / earnings) are how much money you get from your work.

❸ Your (expenses / earnings) are the costs you have to pay.

❹ When your expenses are more than your (budget / earnings), you have a problem.

❺ When you earnings are more than your (budget / expenses), you can save money.

C. What do the words in bold mean to you? Complete the sentences.

① What do you **budget** for entertainment?

I budget _____

_____

② Which advertising **campaign** do you like?

I like _____

_____

③ Which food **satisfies** you?

A food that satisfies me _____

_____

④ What's an **option** you have after graduation?

An option I have _____

_____

My eLab ✎

Visit My eLab to complete Vocabulary Review exercises for this chapter.

Before You Read

A. Look at this pie chart. It shows the average amount of time people use different electronic media. How do you compare? Write how much time you spend using each media.

Use of Electronic Media
Average time adults (18⁺) spend with electronic media in 2014 (hours : minutes)

05:24 ■	live and timeshifted TV
02:43 ■	radio
01:25 ■	smart phone
01:06 ■	Internet on a computer
00:13 ■	game console
00:09 ■	DVD / Blu ray
00:07 ■	multimedia device

TIME I SPEND EACH DAY USING ELECTRONIC MEDIA:

_____ game console   _____ smart phone

_____ Internet on a computer   _____ TV

_____ radio

While You Read

B. While you read, compare what the writer says to things you do. Underline those things that are similar.

Three Ways Technology Has Changed our Lives for the Better

synchronizing (v.): happening at the same time

interaction (n.): two or more things' effects on each other

cram (v.): study a lot over a short period of time

exploits (v.): makes full use of something

inventory (n.): a complete list of items

revolutionized (v.): changed radically

Zyana Morris

The alarm wakes you up early in the morning at precisely the time you set it. How did your phone know when to wake you up without a delay? That is technology perfectly
5 **synchronizing** your daily routine. Technology has the ability to streamline schedules. Technology has changed the entire landscape in which we operate. Technology is everywhere from our everyday **interaction** with mobile phones, laptops, and the like, to the involvement of technology in education, fashion and shopping, the healthcare industry and communications to agriculture.

10 1. Technology has changed the way students study and manage their **budgets**. Gone are the days when students used to spend hours reading lengthy chapters and **cram** all the headings and details for an exam. Technology has taken over and computer presentation slides summarizing long chapters are used by most
15 educational institutes nowadays. Technological gadgets and mobile apps help students and teachers alike. Online libraries, **virtual** learning sites, virtual
20 study sessions, and other **options** are common.

Student life revolves around technology. Many students struggle to **maintain** a work/life
25 balance and are constantly hoping for a miracle to help them budget. Apps and various other technological options help students with academic-related **expenses**, accommodation, and having funds for a social night out.

2. Technology has transformed time management.
30 Businesses rely heavily on time management tools to meet deadlines and to **satisfy** customers. Technology removes communication barriers, increases productivity, and **exploits** resources in a much more efficient manner than before.

Nobody likes to read and reply to emails, so why not let an email scheduler do it for you? The need to organize your inbox in a systematic way is a need of every business
35 person. In our highly digitized world, we have effective tools that can save a great deal of time and money, managing **inventory** and finance, social media **campaigns**, and important alerts and reminders. Small businesses benefit from these technological breakthroughs.

3. Technology has **revolutionized** the way we shop.
40 E-business has revolutionized the way we shop today. A smart phone helps you shop from home. Screen time has increased drastically recently and, on average, people spend around ten hours a day interacting with screens. The business model has changed consumers' shopping behaviour.

(366 words)

Morris, Z. (2016). Three ways technology has changed our lives for the better. LightArrow. Retrieved from http://lightarrow.com/3-ways-technology-has-changed-our-lives-for-the-better

After You Read

C. Choose the phrase that best completes each sentence.

1. Technology can help you streamline _____.
   a) your friends
   b) your fitness
   c) your schedule

2. Technological gadgets and mobile apps help _____.
   a) mostly students
   b) students and teachers
   c) mostly teachers

3. Apps can help students budget their academic expenses and _____.
   a) accommodation and social expenses
   b) common day and night expenses
   c) expenses related to non-academic work

4. Technology removes communication barriers through _____.
   a) email and time management software
   b) people sharing the same phones
   c) computers that automatically talk

5. An email scheduler can save _____.
   a) old unread emails
   b) dates on your calendar
   c) time and money

6. People spend around _____ interacting with screens.
   a) one hundred hours a week
   b) ten hours a day
   c) ten hours a month

D. Review the similarities you underlined in Reading 3 for task B. Fill in the table by writing examples of what you do in terms of budget, time management, or shopping. Compare your answers with a partner.

TECHNOLOGY CHANGE	SIMILARITIES TO WHAT YOU DO
budget	
time management	
shopping	

Working with Others

Working with others can sometimes be difficult, but there are ways to improve that experience. Here are seven simple tips to make working in groups more effective and more efficient (a better use of your time).

A. Read the tips and indicate which ones you already do and which ones you should do.

TIPS FOR WORKING WITH OTHERS	ALREADY DO	SHOULD DO
❶ Get contact information from each group member.		
❷ Schedule meetings, and be on time.		
❸ Recognize each member's strengths and weaknesses.		
❹ Share points of view by asking questions and listening carefully.		
❺ Phrase suggestions as questions.		
❻ Make decisions together, as a group.		
❼ Let others know when they do a good job.		

B. Read these statements. Then review the tips in task A and write the number of the tip that would solve the problem.

_____ I don't know how to get hold of my partner!

_____ I like to write the notes, but I'm not that good at it.

_____ I can't remember what Robin said. I should have asked her what she meant.

_____ I think we'll meet after lunch, but I'm not sure.

_____ I wish he would ask me. Instead he just suggests everything.

_____ No one understands how much work I do.

_____ Peter always tells everyone what to do.

C. Do you have any other tips for working with others? Write them below and then discuss in a group.

_____

_____

_____

_____

FINAL ASSIGNMENT
Write a Comparison Paragraph

Use what you learned in this chapter to write a comparison paragraph. Choose either the block or the point-by-point method.

A. Use your Venn diagram choices and your sentences from the Warm-Up Assignment. Build on what you learned in Focus on Writing (page 94). Begin with a topic sentence and continue with points of comparison.

> Example: This is a comparison of life before and after a long-term power outage. Before an outage, people would take buses. After an outage, people are going to walk most places. But both before and after an outage, some people will ride horses.

B. Refer to the Models Chapter (page 167) to see an example of a comparison paragraph and to learn more about how to write one.

C. Write a draft of your paragraph. Write one sentence in the future tense with *will* and one with *be going to* (refer to Focus on Grammar, page 89). Use comparative and superlative adjectives (see Focus on Reading, page 84). Write a conclusion about how technology might change or be disrupted by other technologies.

> Example: Life in the future **will** be **more difficult than** in the past. Most people **won't** have enough food. Also, farmers **are going to** work **harder** to produce food without electrical machines.

D. You received feedback on your Warm-Up Assignment from your teacher and classmates. Use this feedback to consider how you can improve your writing.

E. Proofread your paragraph. Check your spelling and grammar. Make corrections and write a final copy.

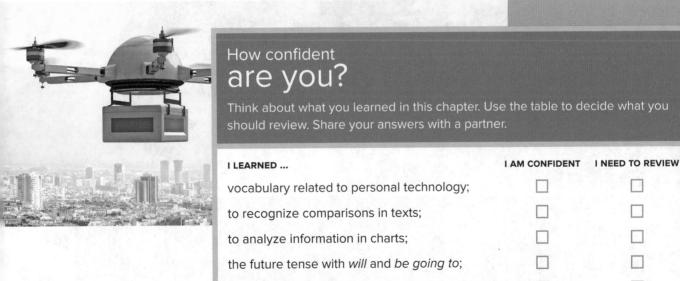

How confident are you?

Think about what you learned in this chapter. Use the table to decide what you should review. Share your answers with a partner.

I LEARNED ...	I AM CONFIDENT	I NEED TO REVIEW
vocabulary related to personal technology;	☐	☐
to recognize comparisons in texts;	☐	☐
to analyze information in charts;	☐	☐
the future tense with *will* and *be going to*;	☐	☐
block and point-by-point methods of comparison;	☐	☐
ways to work with others;	☐	☐
how to create a Venn diagram and write a comparison paragraph.	☐	☐

My eLab ✎
Visit My eLab to build on what you learned.

CHAPTER 6

Living Codes

What makes you the way you are? It is a difficult question to answer. In 1953, James Watson and Francis Crick discovered the structure of DNA. That discovery gave scientists a way to explore how your DNA code can influence your character traits and personality. Other influences include the way you are raised and your environment—the people, things, and events around you. How much do each of these factors affect the decisions you make in life?

In this chapter,
you will

- learn vocabulary related to character traits and personality;

- recognize the main purpose of a text;

- identify facts and opinions;

- review gerunds and infinitives;

- learn note-taking skills;

- create a table with facts and opinions and write an opinion paragraph.

GEARING UP

A. Look at the photo and then answer the questions. *Proactive* means you take steps before a problem occurs. *Reactive* means you wait until a problem occurs before you do something about it.

Proactive and Reactive Choices

1 Are you generally more proactive or more reactive?

_____

2 Proactive people set goals. What goal did you recently set for yourself?

_____

_____

3 Proactive people cannot prepare for everything. Write one example of something you can't prepare for.

_____

_____

4 Reactive people may be better at making quick decisions. Which quick decision did you recently make?

_____

_____

B. Discuss the questions and your answers, first with a partner, then in a group.

Below are the key words you will practise in this chapter. Check the words you understand and then underline the words you use.

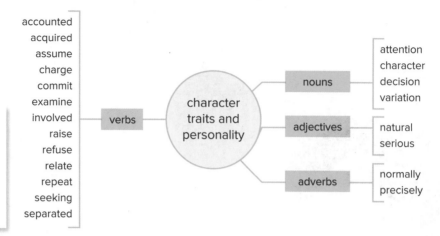

These words are from the Longman Communication 3000 and the Academic Word List. See Appendix 1, page 172.

verbs:
accounted
acquired
assume
charge
commit
examine
involved
raise
refuse
relate
repeat
seeking
separated

character traits and personality

nouns:
attention
character
decision
variation

adjectives:
natural
serious

adverbs:
normally
precisely

FOCUS ON READING

Recognizing the Main Purpose of a Text

Every text has a purpose. For example, the purpose of a bus schedule is to inform. The purpose of a political poster is to persuade. Other types of text are written for other purposes. Knowing the main purpose of a text helps you better understand the message.

A. Match each main purpose to its explanation and example.

MAIN PURPOSES		EXPLANATIONS AND EXAMPLES
❶ to describe	_____	a) point out reasons something is wrong: unfair university fees
❷ to entertain	_____	b) explain how to do something: a recipe
❸ to inform	_____	c) give an idea of what something is like: a photograph
❹ to instruct	_____	d) make you aware of something new: a new rule or law
❺ to persuade	_____	e) make you smile or laugh: a joke or humorous story
❻ to criticize	_____	f) encourage you to do something: an advertisement for a new product or service

Sometimes the purpose of a text is obvious. For example, you can expect documents published by governments to inform or to shape public opinion and behaviour, such as pointing out ways to drive more safely. Other times, it is more difficult to recognize the purpose. When you are unsure, ask yourself if the title suggests why the author wrote the text or if you can tell by how the text is organized.

B. Here are the titles of the three readings in this chapter. Do the titles suggest why the author wrote the text? Complete the table. Indicate type of text and main purpose.

TITLES	SUGGESTS WHY THE WRITER WROTE IT	TYPE OF TEXT	MAIN PURPOSE
❶ Are You Shaped by Nature or Nurture?	☐ yes ☐ no	☐ informational ☐ fiction	☐ inform ☐ criticize
❷ Sometimes, Winners Should Quit	☐ yes ☐ no	☐ entertainment ☐ opinion	☐ persuade ☐ describe
❸ Authors Reveal Algorithms to Live By	☐ yes ☐ no	☐ comparison ☐ explanation	☐ entertain ☐ inform

FOCUS ON CRITICAL THINKING

🛈 Facts are often presented in the present tense.

Identifying Facts and Opinions

When you read a text, think about whether you are reading facts, opinions, or valid opinions. This will help you decide whether you can trust what an author writes.

Facts are researched and usually proven with evidence. We accept some facts that we can't prove because there are logical arguments that support them. For example, looking at the evidence, it is logical that dinosaurs once existed. An author does not need to show you a living dinosaur to have you accept the idea.

Opinions are what an author thinks or feels about a subject. For example, if he or she writes that scientists should bring back dinosaurs, that is the author's opinion. Others may have the opposite opinion. You can argue about opinions, but you cannot argue about facts.

Valid opinions are supported by facts. For example, an author may have the opinion that dinosaurs could be created today and support that opinion with a fact: modern birds are distant relatives of dinosaurs, with similar genetic codes. A valid opinion carries more weight than an opinion without the support of a fact.

A. Indicate whether each statement is a fact, an opinion, or a valid opinion.

STATEMENTS	FACT	OPINION	VALID OPINION
❶ They believe that people are the product of the care and education they receive.			
❷ For many reasons, including hospital mix-ups, identical twins are sometimes separated.			
❸ You may be a certain way because of who your parents were, but how they raise you is just as important in making you who you are.			
❹ Maybe your heroes should be the people who know when to give up.			
❺ Separated twins are likely to become close friends, as an article by Lewis points out.			

B. Some words signal that a statement is a fact or that it is an opinion. Underline words that suggest a fact and highlight words that suggest an opinion. For words you are not sure of, use a dictionary.

believe	exactly	might	percent
possible	probably	proof	seem

READING ❶ Are You Shaped by Nature or Nurture?

Reading 1 begins with the story of two boys who look alike, as if they were identical twins. They come from different backgrounds and the story asks if nature (the traits each were born with) is a more important factor than nurture (the way each was brought up). It's a question scientists keep trying to answer.

VOCABULARY BUILD

In the following exercises, explore key words from Reading 1.

A. Choose the word or phrase that has the closest meaning to the word in bold.

❶ The boy's **decisions** turn out to be wise ones.
   a) choices   b) arguments   c) regrets

❷ Nature and nurture each **accounted** for about 50 percent of a person's personality.
   a) lost   b) examined   c) made up

❸ She missed her chance and cannot **repeat** her test.
   a) do after   b) do again   c) do before

❹ Identical twins are sometimes **separated** at birth.
   a) fixed in place   b) set apart   c) joined together

❺ Are some people born with good **character** and intelligence?
   a) personality   b) reference   c) lettering

B. Words like *charge* and *raise* can be used as nouns or as verbs. Fill in the blanks to complete the sentences. Each word is used twice.

❶ For her good work, her company gave her a _____.

❷ No one else was in _____ of the project.

❸ Make sure you _____ your phone before you go.

❹ If you have a question, _____ your hand.

C. What do the words in bold mean to you? Complete the sentences.

❶ What experience did you have that you would like to **repeat**?

   I would like to repeat _____

   _____

2 What is an important quality in your **character**?

An important quality is _____

_____

3 What's a **decision** you made recently?

I decided to _____

_____

4 What would you do if you were **separated** from a friend in a crowd?

If a friend and I were separated _____

_____

Before You Read

A. Read the title and skim the first and last paragraph. What is the purpose of this text?

☐ to criticize opinions about the differences between pairs of twins

☐ to explain why twins are more likely to be shaped by nurture

☐ to inform readers of the different nature and nurture influences

B. Twins often have many similarities beyond appearance. Read statements about the similarities of twins who were separated when they were one month old. Indicate whether you think each statement is true or false.

STATEMENTS	TRUE	FALSE
1 They had the same kind of headaches.		
2 They had the same habit of biting their nails.		
3 They smoked the same cigarettes.		
4 They drove the same type of car.		
5 They vacationed at the same beach in Florida.		
6 They married women with the same name.		

While You Read

C. While you read, underline facts and highlight opinions.

Are You Shaped by Nature or Nurture?

In the Mark Twain novel, *The Prince and the Pauper*, two boys are born on the same day but **raised** quite differently. One is a poor boy, who is mistreated by his father. The other is Prince Edward, the future King of England. They meet and decide to
5 switch places as a joke. But before the young prince can return to the castle, the poor boy is forced into making important **decisions**. The boy's decisions turn out to be wise ones, based on his **character** not his training. For example, ordering the release of a woman **charged** with being a witch when she cannot **repeat** her crime, that of "causing a storm."

10 The story reflects an old question of whether you are shaped by nature or nurture. Are some people born with good characters and high intelligence? Is the opposite also true, that some
15 people are born with bad characters and low intelligence? In the opinion of the nature supporters, the answer to the questions is "yes." Those who support the nurture argument have
20 the opposite view. They believe that people are the product of the care and education they receive. With the right care and education, they can rise above their circumstances.

25 It's difficult to say one opinion is more **valid** than the other. After all, how could you prove it? It turns out there is a scientific way to examine the question. For many reasons, including hospital **mix-ups**, identical twins are sometimes **separated**. In an unusual case, two pairs of identical twins were separated in Colombia.
30 One of each pair ended up in the countryside and the other of each pair ended up in the capital city, Bogota. Their lives and educations were very different and they had much different jobs, but many of their **habits**, interests, and **personality traits** were similar.

Among the most famous of separated twins are Jim Lewis and Jim Springer. Different
35 families in Ohio, USA, raised them from the time they were a month old. When they met again at age thirty-nine, they discovered they had the same kind of headaches, the same habit of biting their nails, smoked the same cigarettes, drove the same type of car, and vacationed at the same beach in Florida. They married women with the same name, divorced, and married other women with the same name.

40 Many people feel our genes shape us, based on research on similar twin traits such as gun ownership, voting preferences, **job satisfaction**, coffee consumption, and attitudes toward rules. Is it proof that you do not really have a choice about who you become?

In 2015, a team led by Tinca Polderman reviewed fifty years of studies into similarities and differences between twins. They found that, on average, nature and nurture each
45 **accounted** for about 50 percent of a person's personality. So, you may be a certain way because of who your parents were, but how they raise you is just as important in making you who you are. You can make the choice to be a prince or a pauper.

(492 words)

References

Dominus, S. (2015, July 9). The mixed-up brothe_____ ___. _New York Times Magazine._

Lewis, T. (2014, August 11). Tw_____ g_ ring influence of genetics. _LiveScience._ Retrieved from http://www.li_____ -i_ portance-of-genetics.html

Polderman, T.J., Benyamin, _____ _an Bochoven, A., Visscher, P.M. and Posthuma, D. (2015). Meta-a_____ __its based on fifty years of twin studies. _Nature Genetics (47)_ 702–7__

After You Read

D. Choose the phrase that best completes each sentence, according to the text.

1 *The Prince and the Pauper* is about _____.

    a) how some people get to make important decisions

    b) how character may be more important than training

    c) how training may be more important than character

2 If some people are born with good character and high intelligence it suggests _____.

    a) most people are in the middle and are quite normal

    b) we cannot know what other people are like without various tests

    c) some people are born with bad character and low intelligence

3 Separated twins provide the opportunity to _____.

    a) conduct scientific research

    b) share personal opinions

    c) argue about valid opinions

4 Gun ownership, voting preferences, job satisfaction, coffee consumption, and attitudes toward rules are examples of _____.

    a) behaviours that are not shared between twins

    b) surprising similarities between separated twins

    c) issues that have not been researched by twins

5 The Polderman study is important because it explains that _____.

    a) we are mostly influenced by nature

    b) we are mostly influenced by nurture

    c) nature and nurture have equal roles

E. Indicate whether each of these statements from the text is a fact, an opinion, or a valid opinion.

STATEMENTS	FACT	OPINION	VALID OPINION
1 In the Mark Twain novel, *The Prince and the Pauper*, two boys are born on the same day but raised quite differently.			
2 They believe that people are the product of the care and education they receive.			
3 It's difficult to say one opinion is more valid than the other.			
4 Different families in Ohio, USA, raised them from the time they were a month old.			
5 Many people feel our genes shape us, based on research on similar twin traits.			
6 They found that, on average, nature and nurture each accounted for about 50 percent of a person's personality.			

FOCUS ON GRAMMAR

Gerunds and Infinitives

A gerund (verb + -*ing*) is used as a noun that can function as a subject or as the object of certain verbs.

Examples: **Cycling** is good exercise. (subject)
Most people like **cycling**. (object)

A. Draw an arrow ↓ to indicate where the gerund in parentheses should be placed in each sentence.

1 (talking) He liked to her .

3 (working) She liked at the new office .

4 (getting up) Something he does not like is .

5 (swimming) Her favourite sport is .

6 (asking) for help is something everyone should do .

You can decide whether to use a gerund or an infinitive based on the verbs they follow.

An infinitive (*to* + verb) is used as a noun that can also function as a subject or as the object of certain verbs.

Examples: **To quit** is to give up. (subject)
He could not afford **to quit**. (object)

Common verbs that are followed by gerunds or infinitives include: *begin, like, love, prefer,* and *start.* To see a list of verbs followed by gerunds or by infinitives, visit My eLab Documents.

B. Fill in the blanks with the correct form of the verb in parentheses. Use the gerund or the infinitive.

1 He still likes (work) _____*working/to work*_____ at the new bicycle shop.

2 She was unsure what game they wanted (play) _____.

3 How do you like (speak) _____ English every day?

4 He didn't need (work) _____ late.

5 In an emergency, she likes (help) _____.

6 My friend will go (climb) _____ in the Alps.

7 (win) _____ means everything to him.

8 (swim) _____ is something she learned as a child.

My eLab 🖉

Visit My eLab to complete Grammar Review exercises for this chapter.

READING ② Some Winners Know When to Quit

At forty-three, journalist Jean-Dominique Bauby had a stroke that knocked him out. He woke twenty days later, unable to speak and only able to move his left eyelid. But his mind still worked and he wanted to use it. As a friend read the alphabet, Bauby blinked when he heard the letter he wanted. In this way, letter-by-letter, he wrote a book titled *The Diving Bell and the Butterfly.* Many people give up when they face a problem. Others never give up.

In the following exercises, explore key words from Reading 2.

A. Choose the synonym of each word. For words you are not sure of, look at the context (the surrounding words) of the word in Reading 2 for clues. Use a dictionary to check your answers.

1. acquired   a) got   b) lost

2. refuse   a) agree   b) disagree

3. relate   a) connect   b) reject

4. seeking   a) ignoring   b) looking for

B. Scan Reading 2 to find each of these words. Look at the context to help you understand the meaning. Write a definition for each one. For words you are not sure of, use a dictionary.

1. attention: _____

2. involved: _____

3. natural: _____

C. What do the words in bold mean to you? Complete the sentences.

1. What activity would you like to be **involved** in?

   I'd like to be involved in _____

2. Is there a food you **refuse** to eat?

   I refuse to eat _____

3. What is something that holds your **attention**?

   Something that holds my attention is _____

4. What is something you recently **acquired**?

   I recently acquired _____

5. Who is a famous person you can **relate** to?

   I can relate to _____

Before You Read

A. Here is a brief description of C. Robert Cloninger's model of inherited personality traits from the reading. Mark on each scale where you would put yourself. Then compare your answers with a partner.

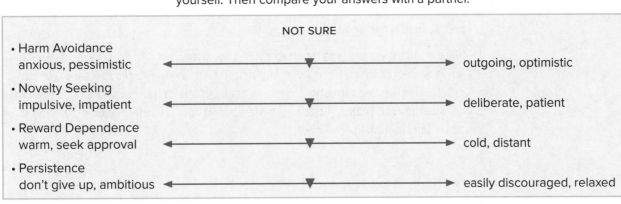

NOT SURE

- Harm Avoidance
  anxious, pessimistic   ⟷   outgoing, optimistic

- Novelty Seeking
  impulsive, impatient   ⟷   deliberate, patient

- Reward Dependence
  warm, seek approval   ⟷   cold, distant

- Persistence
  don't give up, ambitious   ⟷   easily discouraged, relaxed

B. What is the most difficult thing you have done, when you wanted to quit? What made you keep working to reach your goal? Discuss in a group.

While You Read

C. While you read, underline facts and highlight opinions.

Some Winners Know When to Quit

unconquered (adj.): undefeated

fate (n.): the course your life will take

Some people will not quit. William Henley (1849–1903) was sick from childhood. The eldest of six children, he came from a poor family and his father died when he was young. He could not afford to quit. When his illness led to the loss of one of his 5 legs, he did not give up. He wrote the poem "Invictus," which means *unconquered*. The poem ends with, "I am the master of my *fate*, I am the captain of my soul."

Henley's poem was a favourite of another person who also refused to quit—Nelson Mandela. Even after having spent twenty-seven years in jail, Mandela became President of South Africa.

10 Is there a special quality in people who **refuse** to stop? Is it a characteristic that is **acquired**, or is it a **natural** trait, born in some people but not in others? C. Robert Cloninger is a geneticist and 15 expert on mental health. His writing includes a model that describes inherited personality traits, including persistence, the quality of not quitting.

- Harm avoidance: Are you anxious 20 and pessimistic or outgoing and optimistic?

- Novelty **seeking** (looking for new experiences): Are you impulsive and impatient or deliberate and patient?

25 • Reward dependence: Are you warm and seek others' approval or cold and act in a distant way?

- Persistence: Do you not give up and are ambitious or easily discouraged and relaxed?

30 Cloninger's research found these traits directly **relate** to the nature of people's brains. He also identified three other factors about how self-directed, cooperative, and spiritual people are. The last one has to do with whether a person's outlook on life puts other people first versus focusing on material things.

It is easy to list people who have persisted and succeeded against great odds. Japanese 35 businessman Soichiro Honda grew up helping in his family's bicycle shop. He moved to Tokyo and became **involved** in racing cars, but after a terrible accident, he switched his **attention** to making motorcycles and then cars. Honda became a multi-billion dollar international company.

unfit (adj.): not of the quality or standard for a certain purpose

dominate (v.): have control over

heroes (n.): people you look up to

American Oprah Winfrey ran away from home at age fourteen. She eventually found
40 work as a TV news reporter on the evening news, but was fired at age twenty-two and told she was "**unfit** for TV." She started working on a morning talk show and went on to **dominate** daytime TV for twenty-five years.

But do these two examples really show persistence? It depends on your point of view. After all, Honda gave up his dream of being a race car driver and Winfrey did not
45 persist at trying to be an evening news reporter; she only succeeded when she started *another* job in TV. Maybe our **heroes** should be the people who know when to give up. Sometimes winners know when to quit.

(453 words)

Reference

Meriwether, D. (2013, May 19). Is perseverance a partly natural trait? *Quora*. Retrieved from https://www.quora.com/Is-perseverance-a-partly-natural-trait

After You Read

D. This text has more than one purpose. Check all that apply. Discuss your answers with a partner.

☐ to describe ☐ to inform ☐ to persuade

☐ to entertain ☐ to instruct ☐ to criticize

E. Match each person to what he or she did, according to the text.

PEOPLE		WHAT THEY DID
William Henley	_____	a) refused to quit, even after twenty-seven years in jail
Nelson Mandela	_____	b) grew up helping in his family's bicycle shop
C. Robert Cloninger	_____	c) wrote a model that describes inherited personality traits
Soichiro Honda	_____	d) started working on a morning talk show
Oprah Winfrey	_____	e) could not afford to quit

F. What does the author say about persistence in the first and last paragraph? Write your answers, then discuss with a partner.

FIRST PARAGRAPH: _____

_____

FINAL PARAGRAPH: _____

_____

WARM-UP ASSIGNMENT

Write a Table of Facts and Opinions

In this Warm-Up Assignment you will fill in a table with facts and opinions about the influences of nature or nurture. You will use this information to write an opinion paragraph in the Final Assignment.

A. Review the facts that you underlined and the opinions that you highlighted in Reading 1 and Reading 2. Then complete this table. Add other facts and valid opinions you may know.

OPINIONS	*People are shaped by nature.*	*People are shaped by nurture.*
FACTS	*Studies of separated twins show they develop similar habits.*	
VALID OPINIONS	Learning is mostly about your nature because _____ _____ _____ _____	Learning is mostly about your nurture because _____ _____ _____ _____

B. Review the points in your table. Check your spelling and grammar.

C. Read your points aloud. Are there any other errors? Make corrections and write your final copy. Share your table with a partner.

> ❶ Use feedback from your teacher and classmates on this Warm-Up Assignment to improve your writing.

Academic
Survival Skill

Taking Notes

Note taking is a way to help you remember what you read. Start by identifying the most important and most difficult points. These points may include new vocabulary. Use a highlighter, or a pen or pencil, to indicate the key points, such as:

- main ideas;
- questions;
- how the information relates to you or your task;
- new vocabulary and expressions.

A. Read this excerpt from Reading 3. Highlight and label examples of the four key points.

> The new becomes old quickly in today's tech-savvy age. Ready to buy a new phone? Consider how long your current phone might last before another takes its place. The Copernican Principle is a variation on the "where are we in the universe" question astronomer Nicolaus Copernicus asked. It provides the best guess at how much longer something will last. Copernicus' answer was "we are nowhere special," so it follows that ==we are nowhere special in the lifespan of an object at== ← main idea ==any given moment== too.

B. Now, write notes beside each point that show the reason why you highlighted each one. Use short forms, such as *imp.* for *important*, *dif.* for *difficult*, *v.* for *vocabulary*.

C. The final steps in note taking are to write the key points in your own words and then study them. Below are difficult words and expressions, and their definitions. Add notes that help you understand and remember each one.

Nicolaus Copernicus
(1473–1543)

NEW WORDS	DEFINITIONS	NOTES
astronomer	someone who studies things outside the Earth's atmosphere	
best guess	most someone can know about something	
lifespan	how long something lasts for	
tech-savvy	knowledgeable about technology	
universe	everything, including all stars and planets	
variation	different version of something	

READING ❸ **Authors Reveal Algorithms to Live By**

How do you make decisions? Most people make decisions influenced by their emotions. But is there a better way? Brian Christian and Tom Griffiths have found algorithms—number-based processes or formulas—that you can use to improve your decision making.

In the following exercises, explore key words from Reading 3.

A. Fill in the blanks with the correct words to complete the paragraph.

| normally | precisely | serious | variation |

You _____
make many _____
decisions. But when you are young
and need to make decisions
about your education, it is hard
to know _____ what
you will want to do in ten, twenty,
or thirty years. In any case, you
will probably end up doing a
_____ of what you
thought was your perfect job.

B. Match each word to its definition.

WORDS		DEFINITIONS
❶ assume (v.)	_____	a) important
❷ commit (v.)	_____	b) decide to do something
❸ examine (v.)	_____	c) think that you know something
❹ serious (adj.)	_____	d) look at carefully

C. What do the words in bold mean to you? Complete the sentences.

❶ What do you **assume** you will do in five years?

I assume I will _____

_____

❷ What is a piece of art you would like to **examine**?

I'd like to examine _____

❸ What is a **serious** article you have read lately?

I have read _____

❹ What's a **variation** in your daily routine?

A variation in my routine is _____

My eLab
Visit My eLab to complete
Vocabulary Review exercises
for this chapter.

Before You Read

A. How do you solve problems? Below are seven common steps. Number the steps in order. Then discuss with a partner how you could apply these steps to a recent problem.

_____ define the problem

_____ assess the remaining options

_____ brainstorm options

_____ choose the best option

_____ evaluate your success in solving the problem

_____ narrow the options to the best ones

_____ try it

B. Reading 3 describes four situations in which people might have difficulty making a decision. Read the problems. Write notes for your solution to each one.

PROBLEMS	SOLUTIONS
❶ How should you deal with your desk if it is always covered in papers?	
❷ How long should you look before renting or buying an apartment?	
❸ How can you decide when you should find someone to marry?	
❹ How long should you wait before buying a new model of something, like a phone?	

While You Read

C. Apply the note-taking strategies from Academic Survival Skill (page 114). Use a highlighter, or a pen or pencil to indicate main ideas, questions, points that relate to you, and new vocabulary.

Authors Reveal Algorithms to Live By

Jonathan Forani

In Algorithms to Live By: The Computer Science of Human Decisions, academics Brian Christian and Tom Griffiths explain that the human mind is more robotic than we think.

5 When they began to **examine** questions of human decision making, what they found was reassuring. "We get a **justification** for a lot of the things that we consider human ways of making a decision," Christian says. "Like that instinct to pile your papers sloppily on your desk, or to keep looking for a little bit before choosing what apartment to rent, or at what restaurant to dine. We're already doing it right much of the time."

10 Here are four examples of scenarios in which humans can use algorithms to solve problems.

justification (n.): showing something to be right or reasonable

short of knowing (v.): without being able to understand

potential (adj.): having the chance to grow into something

daters (n.): people looking to spend time with others for romantic reasons

concedes (v.): admits something is true

Desk clutter

Algorithm: move-to-front

Organize papers in a pile, and each time one is used, simply put it back on top of the
15 pile. The most recently used information is the information that's most likely to be needed next. "We would **normally** look at a giant stack of papers like that and feel guilty, or feel that we should get organized. The move-to-front rule was proved to be the best, **short of knowing** the future," says Christian.

Apartment hunt

20 *Algorithm: 37 percent rule*

Here's a useful percentage for house hunters: 37 percent. That's the amount of time for a house hunt. If a **potential** buyer has one month to find a new place, Christian and Griffiths suggest waiting eleven days. "After that point, you should **commit** to the first place you see that's better than what you saw in the first 37 percent of your
25 search," says Christian.

Dating

Algorithm: look-then-leap rule

The 37 percent rule takes form in the look-then-leap rule: look for 37 percent of the time, and then leap at the next best thing. If **daters** give
30 themselves from age eighteen to forty to find a mate, they should prepare to leap at age twenty-six. Though, say Christian and Griffiths, the rule isn't as effective in dating as it is in house hunting. "It **precisely** defines the point at which you make a switch from dating being fun, to dating being **serious**," says Christian, who **concedes** that it doesn't always work.

35 ## Duration

Algorithm: Copernican Principle

The new becomes old quickly in today's tech-savvy age. Ready to buy a new phone? Consider how long your current phone might last before another takes its place. The Copernican Principle is a **variation** on the
40 "where are we in the universe" question astronomer Nicolaus Copernicus asked. It provides the best guess for how much longer something will last. Copernicus' answer was "we are nowhere special," so it follows that we are nowhere special in the lifespan of an object at any given moment too.

By this reasoning, any moment in time is as likely as another, so it is safe to **assume**
45 you are halfway through the lifespan of something. For example, Google, founded in 1998, should be around until about 2034.

(490 words)

Forani, J. (2016, June 7). Authors reveal 'Algorithms to Live By.' *The Toronto Star*. Retrieved from https://www.thestar.com/life/2016/06/07/authors-reveal-algorithms-to-live-by.html

After You Read

D. Connect the phrases to summarize Reading 3.

SUMMARY		
❶ Brian Christian and Tom Griffiths ...	_____	a) for piles of paper is best.
❷ The book is about ...	_____	b) of an object at any given moment.
❸ The human mind is ...	_____	c) always work for dating.
❹ We're already making the right ...	_____	d) more robotic than we think.
❺ The move-to-front rule ...	_____	e) to the first place you see.
❻ After eleven days commit ...	_____	f) decisions much of the time.
❼ The 37 percent rule doesn't ...	_____	g) are academics.
❽ We are nowhere special in the lifespan ...	_____	h) how we make decisions.

E. Indicate whether these statements are true or false, according to the text.

STATEMENTS	TRUE	FALSE
❶ Humans use algorithms to make decisions the way robots do.		
❷ Feeling guilty is something that humans and robots both do.		
❸ Committing to a house means that you will buy it.		
❹ The authors suggest that dating is more fun when you use algorithms.		
❺ The Copernican Principle is likely to be used when making the decision of when to buy a new model.		
❻ The phrase "any time is as likely as another," means you should wait as long as possible to make a purchase.		
❼ The authors think Google will last forever.		
❽ A general idea of the book is to trust your decisions.		

F. Check your answers in Before You Read, task B. Now that you have read the text, choose one answer you might change. Write the new answer, then discuss with a partner.

_____

_____

Writing an Opinion Paragraph

When you give an opinion among friends, you do not necessarily need to support it with facts. But when you give an opinion in academic writing, you do need to support it with facts. As you learned in Focus on Critical Thinking (page 105), an opinion supported with facts is a *valid opinion*.

Writing an opinion paragraph starts with choosing a topic and stating an opinion on that topic. Sometimes an opinion is expressed in the title, and sometimes it is expressed in the first sentence.

A. Choose the title and the topic sentence that best express an opinion.

1 TITLE:

☐ I Don't Like Rules

☐ Rules Are Laws You Have to Follow

☐ Don't Live Your Life by Others' Rules

2 TOPIC SENTENCE:

☐ Rules that work for some people may not work as well for others.

☐ What is a rule, anyway?

☐ I don't really know any rules that are important for others or me.

B. An opinion paragraph should include valid opinions. Choose the phrase that best supports each opinion.

1 Organizing a messy desk is not difficult _____.

a) according to a new system of putting your most-used things in front

b) but no one likes to do it because it can take so long

2 The worst thing is to rush to buy a new phone if you do not _____.

a) apply the Copernican Principle

b) find your favourite model and colour

3 It shouldn't be difficult to find a perfect apartment when you _____.

a) are generally a happy person

b) use Christian and Griffiths 37 percent rule

4 It's not impossible to tell identical twins apart _____.

a) because friends will usually know their habits

b) according to a 2011 study that used police dogs

C. At the end of an opinion paragraph, write a sentence that summarizes what you said or that says something new, such as an action people should take. Choose the sentence that best restates the opinion.

☐ I might have the wrong opinion about rules, but it's what I believe.

☐ If you follow rules you don't understand, you will have problems.

☐ Maybe following rules will make you happy, but maybe not.

FINAL ASSIGNMENT
Write an Opinion Paragraph

Use what you learned in this chapter to write an opinion paragraph.

A. Choose which opinion you will write about.

☐ People are shaped by nature. OR ☐ People are shaped by nurture.

B. Build on the information in your table from the Warm-Up Assignment (page 114) to write a draft of your paragraph (see Focus on Writing). Start with a topic sentence. Give the reason for your opinion.

Example: Nature shapes people more than nurture because ...

C. Write sentences that support your opinion, along with facts and valid opinions (refer to Focus on Critical Thinking, page 105). Valid opinions might include commonly accepted facts, as well as facts you've recently read or heard. You could mention a famous person who is an example of the benefits of nature or nurture. Try to use at least one example of a gerund and one example of an infinitive (refer to Focus on Grammar, page 110).

D. Write a conclusion that summarizes your paragraph or makes a suggestion for readers to follow.

E. Use the feedback you received on your Warm-Up Assignment to consider how you can improve your writing. Refer to the Models Chapter (page 168) to see an example of an opinion paragraph and to learn more about how to write one.

F. Proofread your paragraph. Check your spelling, grammar, and punctuation. Did you use a gerund and an infinitive correctly?

G. Read your paragraph aloud. Are there any other errors? Make corrections and write a final copy. Share your paragraph with a partner.

How confident are you?

Think about what you learned in this chapter. Use the table to decide what you should review. Share your answers with a partner.

I LEARNED ...	I AM CONFIDENT	I NEED TO REVIEW
vocabulary related to character traits and personality;	☐	☐
to recognize the main purpose of a text;	☐	☐
to identify facts and opinions;	☐	☐
about gerunds and infinitives;	☐	☐
note-taking skills;	☐	☐
how to create a table with facts and opinions and write an opinion paragraph.	☐	☐

My eLab ✎
Visit My eLab to build on what you learned.

CHAPTER 7
Robots, AI, and the Future

Science fiction books and movies shape your ideas about robots and artificial intelligence (AI). In some cases, robots appear as metal humans, but are stronger and faster. They are frequently evil and plan to take over the world. The same stories are told about AI machines. These machines control weapons and start wars to destroy humans. But most robots and AI programs are neither strong nor intelligent. Are you afraid of robots?

In this chapter,
you will

- learn vocabulary related to robots and artificial intelligence;

- recognize a process in a text;

- identify problems and solutions;

- review prepositions of time;

- describe a process;

- learn how to study smarter;

- write steps in a process and a process paragraph.

GEARING UP

A. Look at the illustration and then answer the questions.

Steps in a Process

1. Before ideas, come problems. What is a problem with robots?

   _____

   _____

2. *Team* and *work* go together. Why is it helpful to work on big ideas as a team?

   _____

   _____

3. *Vision* is about thinking long term. What jobs will robots have in the long term?

   _____

   _____

4. The word *result* is followed by *success*. What step do you take if you don't achieve success?

   _____

   _____

B. Discuss the questions and your answers, first with a partner, then in a group.

Below are the key words you will practise in this chapter. Check the words you understand and then underline the words you use.

These words are from the Longman Communication 3000 and the Academic Word List. See Appendix 1, page 172.

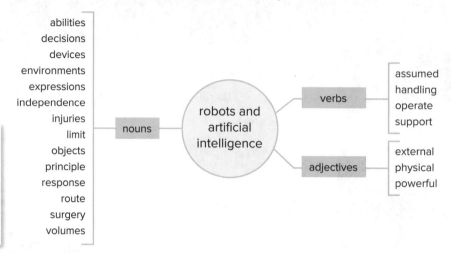

nouns:
abilities
decisions
devices
environments
expressions
independence
injuries
limit
objects
principle
response
route
surgery
volumes

robots and artificial intelligence

verbs:
assumed
handling
operate
support

adjectives:
external
physical
powerful

FOCUS ON READING

Recognizing a Process in a Text

One way to organize ideas is in a series of steps. This is called a *process*. Steps in a process describe how something happens or happened. A process can help you solve a problem, or meet a need. Two common examples of a process are a recipe and a set of instructions, such as how to build something. To recognize a process, look for transition words that show the start of each step. Sometimes transition words are numbers.

A. Fill in the missing transition words in the last column.

NUMERALS	1	2	3
❶ cardinal numbers	one	two	
❷ ordinal numbers	first	second	
❸ ordinal adverbs	firstly	secondly	

B. Look at these words and phrases. Underline the ones that show a first step. Highlight the ones that show a last step.

after	for a start	next
at first	in the end	then
finally	initially	to begin
first of all	lastly	

C. Choose one word or phrase from task B and use it in a sentence.

_____

_____

D. Underline the transition words in this paragraph. There are five.

First, a patient swallows the capsule. Then the capsule reaches the stomach. Next, the ice covering on the capsule quickly melts and the origami robot unfolds itself. Then a doctor steers it with external magnets. These magnets also control how the capsule behaves. The origami robot can swim or even crawl across a stomach wall. Once the robot reaches the button battery, it changes shape so it can pick up the battery. Finally, the robot swims with the battery to exit the body.

origami

FOCUS ON CRITICAL THINKING

Identifying Problems and Solutions

Often a text starts by describing a problem. Then it presents one or more solutions. A problem can be something that has been around for a long time, such as poverty. Or it could be a new problem, such as students spending too much time online. Here are two ways to identify problems and solutions in a text.

• Identify the topic sentence; it may point out the problem and suggest a solution.

• Scan for words that show something is a problem, such as *problem, need, challenge, question,* and *issue*.

A. Read this excerpt from Reading 1. Underline the topic sentence.

button batteries

A new miniature robot might help with the issue of harmful batteries in children's stomachs. Button batteries are used in watches and other small electrical devices. They seem harmless, but they're not. This is because children often swallow them. In the US alone, children swallow 3,500 batteries every year. Once inside the stomach, the batteries can cause damage. Usually, the only way to reach them is through surgery.

B. Read the paragraph again and write the problem in your own words.

_____

_____

_____

_____

READING ❶   **A Robot That You Can Swallow**

You probably think of robots as large machines. But some researchers want to create tiny robots small enough to swim through your blood. That may be years away, but there is a robot that you can swallow. What do you think is the purpose of a robot that you can swallow?

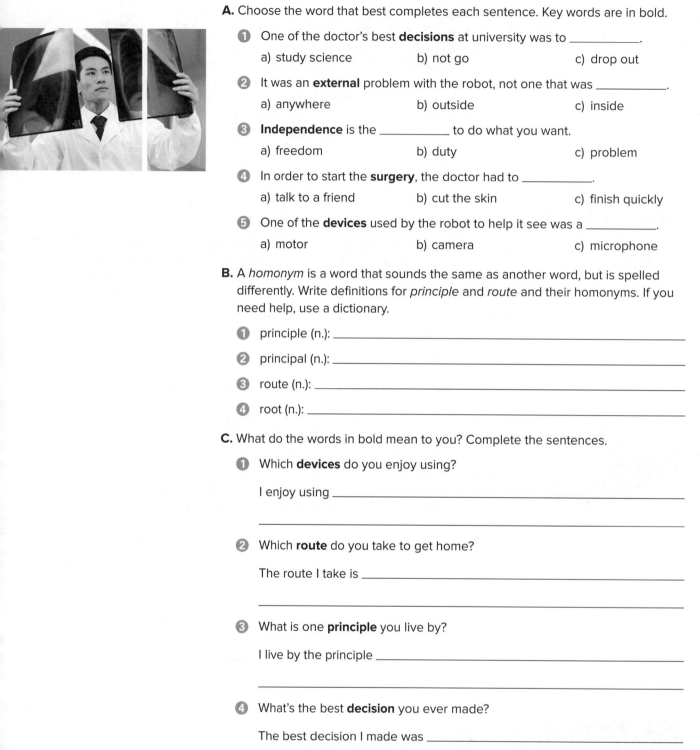

In the following exercises, explore key words from Reading 1.

A. Choose the word that best completes each sentence. Key words are in bold.

1 One of the doctor's best **decisions** at university was to _____.

a) study science   b) not go   c) drop out

2 It was an **external** problem with the robot, not one that was _____.

a) anywhere   b) outside   c) inside

3 **Independence** is the _____ to do what you want.

a) freedom   b) duty   c) problem

4 In order to start the **surgery**, the doctor had to _____.

a) talk to a friend   b) cut the skin   c) finish quickly

5 One of the **devices** used by the robot to help it see was a _____.

a) motor   b) camera   c) microphone

B. A *homonym* is a word that sounds the same as another word, but is spelled differently. Write definitions for *principle* and *route* and their homonyms. If you need help, use a dictionary.

1 principle (n.): _____

2 principal (n.): _____

3 route (n.): _____

4 root (n.): _____

C. What do the words in bold mean to you? Complete the sentences.

1 Which **devices** do you enjoy using?

I enjoy using _____

_____

2 Which **route** do you take to get home?

The route I take is _____

_____

3 What is one **principle** you live by?

I live by the principle _____

_____

4 What's the best **decision** you ever made?

The best decision I made was _____

_____

5 What gives you a feeling of **independence**?

I feel independent when _____

_____

Before You Read

A. In Focus on Critical Thinking, you read how children sometimes swallow small button batteries. You also read that a tiny robot could be swallowed to retrieve them. Why might a small robot be a good solution to the problem? Discuss with a partner.

_____

_____

B. Reading 1 discusses different kinds of robots. Two qualities of robots are intelligence and independence. Intelligence means a robot can make decisions and learn. Independence means it can move from place to place, usually on wheels. Think about a Mars rover, a robot that collects and analyzes samples on Mars. Is it intelligent or independent or both? Discuss with a partner.

While You Read

C. While you read, number the steps in the process on the origami robot diagram on page 128.

A Robot You Can Swallow

stomach (n.): internal organ that digests food

solve (v.): find an answer to a problem

obstacles (n.): things in your way

repetitive (adj.): over and over

A new miniature robot might help with the issue of harmful batteries in children's stomachs. Button batteries are used in watches and other small electrical **devices**. They seem harmless, but they're not. This is because children often swallow them. In
5 the US alone, children swallow 3,500 batteries every year. Once inside the **stomach**, the batteries can cause damage. Usually, the only way to reach them is through **surgery**.

There are three classes of robots. Each level has different degrees of intelligence and **independence**. The smartest class of robots is designed with artificial intelligence (AI) that allows them to make decisions and learn. These include robots that **solve**
10 simple problems like delivering medicines and other packages from one place to another. The Robocourier is one example. It plans its own **route** and goes around **obstacles**. Typically, it travels around a hospital to save time for medical staff. In a large hospital, saving time saves lives.

A second class of robots is programmed to do simple **repetitive** jobs. An example is
15 the Bestic. It's a robot arm that holds a fork or a spoon to help feed people who are unable to feed themselves. It can be controlled with a joystick, buttons, or a foot pedal. This kind of robot is used in hospitals and also in people's homes.

The third class of robots does not do anything on their own; they may move but are just tools, controlled by humans. Among these human-controlled robots is an origami
20 robot. It was developed in 2016 by researchers at MIT, the University of Sheffield, and the Tokyo Institute of Technology. The robot does not actually practise origami— the art of Japanese paper folding. Rather, it uses origami **principles** to fold and unfold. This folding allows it to move and pick up things.

① Vocabulary Tip: A new word like "origami" may be defined in a phrase that follows it, such as in this phrase "origami— the art of Japanese paper folding."

magnets (n.): pieces of iron that attract other pieces of iron

The origami robot is so tiny that it fits inside a capsule—or pill—that is made of ice.
25 First, imagine that at nine o'clock in the morning a hospital patient swallows the capsule. A minute later, the capsule reaches the stomach. Next, the ice covering on the capsule quickly melts and the origami robot unfolds itself. Then a doctor steers it with **external magnets**.
30 These magnets also control the robot. The origami robot can swim or even crawl across a stomach wall. Once the robot reaches the button battery, it changes shape to pick up the battery.
35 Finally, at nine-thirty, the robot swims with the battery to exit the body and the patient goes home.

This kind of robot is so small, there is no room on it for a computer processor
40 that might help it think and make **decisions**. In the future, this might change. Would you swallow a small robot to act like a little doctor in your body, identifying and solving problems?

(463 words)

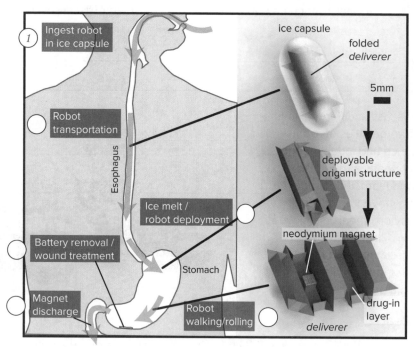

1 Ingest robot in ice capsule

Robot transportation

Esophagus

Ice melt / robot deployment

Battery removal / wound treatment

Stomach

Magnet discharge

Robot walking/rolling

ice capsule

folded *deliverer*

5mm

deployable origami structure

neodymium magnet

drug-in layer

deliverer

Reference

Hardesty, L. (2016, May 12). Ingestible origami robot. *MIT News.* Retrieved from http://news.mit.edu/2016/ingestible-origami-robot-0512

After You Read

D. Indicate whether these statements are true or false, according to the text.

STATEMENTS	TRUE	FALSE
❶ One child swallowed more than 3,500 button batteries.		
❷ The smartest robots use artificial intelligence to learn.		
❸ Some robots only do repetitive jobs.		
❹ Robots are always more than simply tools.		
❺ The origami robot has a computer processor to help it think.		
❻ Someday, swallowed robots may search for and solve problems.		
❼ It's called an origami robot because it unfolds.		
❽ The origami robot is made of ice.		
❾ The patient goes home with the robot still inside.		

E. Show the process by numbering these steps in order. Refer to the diagram in Reading 1 if you need help.

_____ A hospital patient swallows a robot in a capsule.

_____ Then a doctor steers and controls the robot with external magnets.

_____ The robot changes shape to pick up the button battery.

_____ The capsule reaches the stomach.

_____ The origami robot swims or crawls across the stomach wall.

_____ The ice covering on the capsule melts and the origami robot unfolds itself.

_____ The robot swims with the battery to exit the body and the patient goes home.

FOCUS ON GRAMMAR

Prepositions of Time: *At, In, On*

When you read, you see common prepositions of time: *at, in, on*. Each preposition is used for a different purpose:

• *at* is used for an exact time;

• *in* is used for months, years, and other long periods;

• *on* is used for specific days and dates.

A. Fill in the blanks with the correct prepositions of time: *at, in, on*.

❶ It was developed _____ 2016 by researchers.

❷ First, imagine that _____ nine o'clock in the morning a hospital patient swallows the capsule.

❸ Finally, _____ nine-thirty, the robot swims with the battery to exit the body.

❹ _____ 2015, Dr. David Hanson, of Hanson Robotics, built a lifelike robot named Sophia.

❺ At a conference _____ March 17, 2016, Hanson jokingly asked Sophia a question.

❻ _____ Monday, we will have a meeting about building a robot.

B. Some expressions of time also use the prepositions *at, in, on*. Complete these expressions.

❶ _____ the morning

❷ _____ the afternoon

❸ _____ night

❹ _____ Fridays

❺ _____ New Year's Eve

❻ _____ week nights

My eLab

Visit My eLab to complete Grammar Review exercises for this chapter.

READING ② How Do Artificial Intelligence Programs Work?

It's difficult to measure intelligence. Computers with artificial intelligence can do math problems far faster than humans and remember millions of things. But intelligence is a combination of knowledge and using it to solve problems in creative ways. Do you think computers will be as intelligent as people one day?

VOCABULARY BUILD

In the following exercises, explore key words from Reading 2.

A. Match each word to its definition.

WORDS		DEFINITIONS
1 assumed (v.)	_____	a) the way a face shows feelings
2 expressions (n.)	_____	b) written or spoken answer
3 operate (v.)	_____	c) help
4 response (n.)	_____	d) thought something true without proof
5 support (v.)	_____	e) amounts
6 volumes (n.)	_____	f) work

B. What do the words in bold mean to you? Complete the sentences.

1 What is your **limit** for staying up late?

I can stay up until _____

2 How do you **support** your friends?

I support my friends by _____

_____

3 What is your **response** when someone asks to borrow a book?

My response is _____

4 What do you **assume** you will do tonight?

I assume I will _____

Before You Read

A. Sometimes, it can be difficult to identify the problem in a text. Here is the first paragraph of Reading 2. After you read it, choose the sentence that best summarizes the problem.

> Are you afraid of four year olds? Do you think they will take over the world? No? Then you may not need to worry about artificial intelligence (AI). The best AI programs only operate at the level of a four-year-old child. They seem intelligent because they can win at games like chess and make decisions quickly, but they need a lot of support.

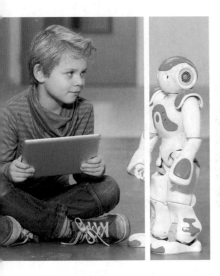

☐ Four year olds may take over the world.

☐ You do not need to worry about artificial intelligence.

☐ AI programs only operate at the level of a four year old.

☐ AI programs are too good at games like chess.

☐ AI programs need a lot of support.

B. How do you think AI works? Choose the statements you think are true and then discuss with a partner.

☐ AI machines learn the same way human babies learn.

☐ AI machines are usually trained for a single task.

☐ AI machines understand what is right and wrong.

☐ AI machines never forget things they learn.

☐ AI machines can be just as smart as people.

While You Read

C. One problem in Reading 2 is how AI systems need support. While you read, underline the transition words that show a process. They will help you understand the limits of artificial intelligence.

How Do Artificial Intelligence Programs Work?

rulebook (n.): regulations to follow

symbols (n.): marks that stand for something else

consulting (adv.): looking for expert advice

Are you afraid of four year olds? Do you think they will take over the world? No? Then you may not need to worry about artificial intelligence (AI). The best AI programs only **operate** at the level of a four-year-old child. They seem intelligent because they
5 can win at games like chess and make decisions quickly, but they need a lot of **support**.

John Searle, a computer scientist, explains the **limits** of AI in a story he calls "The Chinese Room." The room is used for answering questions in Chinese. Here are five steps you need to follow.

First, you take a piece of paper and write a question in Chinese and put it through a
10 small hole next to the door.

Second, the person inside the room takes the paper and compares the Chinese characters to ones in books in the room.

Third, the person consults a **rulebook**. The rulebook says things like, "When you see X symbol(s), reply with Y **symbols**."

15 Fourth, the person follows the instructions and pushes the answer back through the hole next to the door.

Fifth, you look at the person's answer and check it. If it does not answer your question, you try again, perhaps asking your question another way. When the **response** answers your question, you are finished.

20 After getting a correct answer, you probably **assumed** that the person in the room was a Chinese speaker and perhaps even an intelligent one. However, the conclusion would be false. Instead, the story shows how computers seem intelligent when they are simply **consulting** rules and large **volumes** of information. The computer making these calculations is not intelligent.

accurate (adj.): correct in all details

jokingly (adv.): in a humorous way

25 Could this change? Yes, of course. In time, access to huge amounts of data and more sophisticated rules might give AI machines the ability to solve problems and do more of the thinking jobs that humans do. For 30 example, AI is already used to mark student essays and is more **accurate** than human markers. This is because human markers get tired. They may give the same paper two different marks depending on the 35 time of day they look at it. A computer AI program never gets tired.

In 2015, Dr. David Hanson, of Hanson Robotics, built a lifelike AI robot named Sophia. Sophia's face can show dozens of different **expressions** and her eyes are cameras. She uses computer processers to help her understand what people say. She responds 40 in a human-like voice.

It sounds impressive, but the key problem is not the thinking ability of an AI machine. It is giving robots control over important decisions. In such cases, a mistaken rule or incorrect data might encourage the AI robot to harm humans. At a conference, on March 17, 2016, Hanson **jokingly** asked Sophia a question, "Do you want to destroy 45 humans? Please say no."

Sophia replied, "Okay, I will destroy humans."

In the end, Sophia has a lot to learn.

(485 words)

References

Anderson, D.L. (2006). Searle and the Chinese Room Argument. *Consortium on Cognitive Science Instruction*. Retrieved from http://www.mind.ilstu.edu/curriculum/searle_chinese_room/searle_chinese_room.php

Taylor, H. (2016, March 16). Could you fall in love with this robot? *CNBC*. Retrieved from http://www.cnbc.com/2016/03/16/could-you-fall-in-love-with-this-robot.html

After You Read

D. Choose the phrase that best completes each sentence, according to the text.

❶ AI is compared to a four year old because they both _____.

a) have a sense of playfulness

b) have a similar level of intelligence

c) are unlikely to organize themselves

❷ John Searle's Chinese Room is an example of how _____.

a) to get free translations

b) the Internet learns Chinese

c) AI processes information

3 As AI machines learn more, they are likely to _____.

    a) focus on creating robots

    b) take over more human jobs

    c) refuse to work for humans anymore

4 Computers mark essays more accurately because they _____.

    a) don't have favourite students

    b) don't want to be unfair

    c) never get tired

5 Sophia's different expressions make it easier for her to _____.

    a) express emotions

    b) listen to others

    c) understand faces

6 Sophia probably said she would destroy humans because she _____.

    a) is working closely with other AI machines

    b) doesn't understand what the words mean

    c) was joking with inventor Dr. David Hanson

E. Number these steps in the Chinese Room process in the correct order.

_____ You write a question in Chinese and put it through a small hole.

_____ The person returns the answer.

_____ The person uses a rulebook and writes an answer.

_____ You check the answer.

_____ A person in the room compares the Chinese characters to ones in books.

F. Besides the main problem of the limits of AI, other problems are identified in the text. Highlight three sentences that indicate other problems. Then write one of the problems in your own words.

_____

_____

_____

FOCUS ON WRITING

Describing a Process

A process describes how something happened. You can write the steps of a process in a list or in a paragraph. Use these tips to write a process.

• Think about the steps in the process. How many are there?

• Cut out unnecessary information.

• Use transition words to guide the reader from step to step.

• Give examples and explanations when needed.

A. Here is an excerpt from Reading 2. Draw an arrow to connect the notes in blue to the part each refers to.

Start with a sentence that introduces the topic.

Use transition words like ordinal numbers to start each step.

> John Searle, a computer scientist, explains the limits of AI in a story he calls "The Chinese Room." The room is used for answering questions in Chinese. Here are five steps you need to follow.
>
> First, you take a piece of paper and write a question in Chinese and put it through a small hole next to the door.

Give an explanation of anything that might not be clear.

Give the reader an idea of how many steps there are.

B. Look at the photo. A boy's drone hit a woman. Complete the sentences to describe the process of what happened.

- Start with a topic sentence.
- Explain terms the reader might not know.
- Give details of the date and time and what was happening.
- Explain the steps using transition words. Use a transition word for each step.
- Add any other necessary information.

There was a drone accident. A drone is a _____

On _____ at _____, a boy was flying his drone.

First, _____

_____

Then, _____

_____

Finally, _____

_____

The woman was not hurt.

C. Share your answers with a partner. Are your sentences the same or different?

Describing a process is important in business and science.

WARM-UP ASSIGNMENT
Write Steps in a Process

Look at the five photos. An AI system would look at these photos and use a process with rules to decide which one is a balloon.

Example: Look at the first object. If it has more than one hole, it's not a balloon. Look at the second object. If it's flat or has moving parts, it's not a balloon. ...

It is not unusual for an AI system to be more accurate than humans.

A. In this Warm-Up Assignment you will model an AI system. Choose a process that you do that requires four or five steps. The process should involve making decisions. For example, how do you solve the problem of what to do for fun on the weekend? Ask your teacher to approve your choice.

B. Start with what you learned in Focus on Grammar (page 129) to write the time and date.

Example: On September 5, at five o'clock, I decided what to do on the weekend.

C. Write the process steps as a numbered list. Refer to the Models Chapter (page 169) to see an example of steps in a process and to learn more about how to write them.

Example: 1) I checked how much free time I had.

D. Check your process steps.
- ☐ Are all the words spelled correctly?
- ☐ Is your grammar correct?
- ☐ Did you use the correct punctuation?

E. Read your process steps aloud. Are there any other errors? Make corrections and write your final copy.

F. Share your list with a partner.

 Use feedback from your teacher and classmates on this Warm-Up Assignment to improve your writing.

READING ③ — Give Us a Hand: It's Time for Robots to Get Physical

Picking up an egg is a simple task for you. But it is a complicated task for a robot. Too much pressure and the egg is crushed. Too little pressure and the egg falls and cracks. In movies, robots are often human-like, walking and using their hands like humans. But in the real world, scientists struggle to give robots the complex skills necessary to pick up everyday things.

VOCABULARY BUILD

In the following exercises, explore key words from Reading 3.

A. Draw an arrow ↓ to indicate where the word in parentheses should be placed in each sentence.

① (objects) One test for a robot is whether it can move .

② (handling) There are different ways of AI problems .

③ (environments) One of the where robots work is underwater .

④ (abilities) Some robots' include walking .

⑤ (injuries) Some are caused by quickly moving robots .

B. *Antonyms* are words that have the opposite meaning. Underline the antonyms of the adjectives *physical* and *powerful*.

① physical: material mental thoughtful bodily emotional

② powerful: faint feeble strong tired weak

C. What do the words in bold mean to you? Complete the sentences.

① What's a favourite **object** you own?

A favourite object I own _____

_____

② What do you do for **physical** fitness?

For physical fitness, I _____

_____

③ What's the best **environment** for you to study in?

The best environment for me is _____

_____

④ What is one of your technical **abilities**?

One of my technical abilities is _____

_____

My eLab ✎

Visit My eLab to complete Vocabulary Review exercises for this chapter.

Before You Read

A. Look at the four devices on the next page. Each has artificial intelligence. But how are they different? Indicate each device's qualities in the table on page 137 and then discuss with a partner.

voice recognition phone

industrial robot

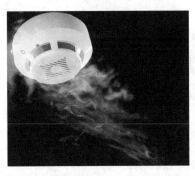

smoke detector

washing machine

DEVICE QUALITIES	PHONE	ROBOT	SMOKE DETECTOR	WASHING MACHINE
1 It is interactive.	✓			
2 It mostly does one job.				
3 It understands spoken commands.				
4 It can learn.				
5 It needs to be programmed for each task.				

While You Read

B. While you read, underline three problems.

Give Us a Hand: It's Time for Robots to Get Physical

outmanoeuvred (adv.): used skill to get an advantage

AlphaGo—a Google computer that plays the game Go—beat Lee Sedol, the world's master of the game. AI once again **outmanoeuvred** us.

Except there's one thing AlphaGo *couldn't* do: pick up those black and white Go stones
5 and put them down on the board. A Google programmer had to do that.

"Maybe the hardest part is not playing the game but moving the pieces," says Siddhartha Srinivasa, a roboticist at Carnegie Mellon University. Srinivasa is an expert in robot manipulation—the art of grabbing, holding, and using **objects**. And this is the real challenge. Robots are increasingly able to understand the world, but they're terrible
10 at **handling** it. If robots are really going to start helping us out in everyday life, they're going to have to be more than smart. They're going to have to become **physical**.

As an example, in the Amazon Picking Challenge, robots had to grab loose objects—like a package of Oreos or a rubber duck—and put them in a container. The winner took twenty minutes to move ten items. The other teams did far worse; a **toddler**
15 could have beaten them all.

The physical world **defeats** robots because it's been designed by and for humans. We're masterful at dealing with mess and uncertainty. We **intuitively** understand the behaviour of stacks and things that roll over on their sides. Robots don't. "Just look at your own desk," Srinivasa says. "It's covered with clutter, because humans are
20 expert at dealing with clutter."

Today's workplace robots—like the ones that move stuff around in Amazon warehouses or the robots that weld parts on automobile assembly lines—work in super-clean structured **environments** designed to accommodate their **powerful** but limited set of **abilities**. When they reach to pick something up, we make sure it's exactly where
25 they expect it to be. And when uncertainty arises, humans have to step in. Mercedes-Benz has lately been replacing some robots with humans because customers increasingly want their cars **customized**—and robots can't do that.

So how can we give these robots a hand? One approach is soft pneumatics, designed to cushion a grab at everyday objects.

30 But do we *want* robots to be nimble enough to fold origami? Machines like that could take over nearly any manual-labor or service job from humans. But they'd also be our helpmates. As Srinivasa points out, millions of people struggle with mobility problems as a result of issues ranging from spinal-cord **injuries** to old age. Robots could help them feed and clothe themselves.

35 Plus, they could finally slap down their own Go pieces.

(428 words)

Thompson, C. (2016, June). Give us a hand: It's time for robots to get physical. *Wired Magazine*. Retrieved from http://www.wired.com/2016/06/robot-body-parts/

After You Read

C. Below are three problems you might have identified in While You Read. Write the solution that the text gives for each problem.

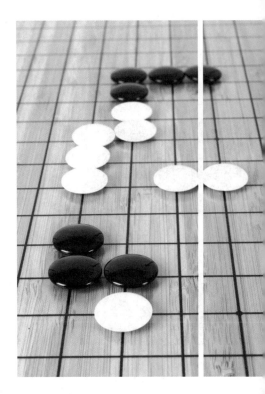

PROBLEMS	SOLUTIONS
❶ AlphaGo couldn't pick up Go stones.	
❷ Robots can't customize cars.	
❸ Millions of people struggle with mobility problems.	

D. Connect the phrases to summarize Reading 3.

SUMMARY		
❶ AlphaGo beat ...	_____	a) become physical.
❷ AlphaGo *couldn't* pick up the Go stones; ...	_____	b) mess and uncertainty.
❸ In order to help us, robots need to ...	_____	c) help with mobility problems.
❹ The Amazon Picking Challenge winner took ...	_____	d) at everyday objects.
❺ Humans are masterful at dealing with ...	_____	e) designed to accommodate their abilities.
❻ Workplace robots work in environments ...	_____	f) the world's master of the game.
❼ Soft pneumatics cushion a grab ...	_____	g) twenty minutes to move ten items.
❽ Robots will become our helpmates and ...	_____	h) a person had to do that.

E. Write one advantage of having machines that could think and move like people.

_____

_____

Academic
Survival Skill

Studying Smarter

Many people think learning ends with school. But you continue to learn throughout your life. This means you continue to study. There are ways to study smarter, using your time more wisely, and remembering more.

A. Read the tips and answer the questions with information that is true for you.

1 **Ask questions:** Begin with questions about what the topic means to you. Think of something you are studying now. Why are you studying this topic? What is important about it? Also ask your teacher questions, such as the format of the test and what will be on it.

I'm studying this topic because _____

_____

I will ask my teacher about _____

_____

2 **Set goals:** It helps to know what you want to accomplish. Your goals can be short-term to help you do something this week, such as to help you understand a new idea. Or your goals can be long-term, such as improving your reading speed. What are your goals?

My short-term goal is _____

My long-term goal is _____

3 **Plan your study time:** Some students only study before a test. But to remember and improve, you need to study regularly. Make studying a routine. At what times and in which places will you study this week?

I will study _____

_____

4 **Find a study partner:** Studying with a partner can help in many ways. You can make sure you have a common understanding of the topic. You can test each other. You can support each other. What are the qualities of a good study partner?

A good study partner should _____

_____

5 **Balance your life:** Some students don't study enough. Other students study too much! Balance your life with regular exercise and good food. Avoid too many breaks where you sit and watch a screen. Play a sport. Go for a walk. How will you balance your studying? Which kind of break will make you feel better?

I can balance my studying by _____

_____

❶ You're not alone. Ask other students and your teacher for study tips.

B. Which of the points in task A do you already do? Which are the most useful? Discuss with a partner.

© **ERPI** • Reproduction prohibited

FINAL ASSIGNMENT
Write a Process Paragraph

Use what you learned in this chapter to rewrite your Warm-Up Assignment process as a paragraph.

A. Use your process steps to write your paragraph.

- Start with a topic sentence that includes the problem.
- Explain terms the reader might not know.
- Write the date and the time. Use the prepositions of time you learned in Focus on Grammar (page 129).
- Explain the steps to solving your problem. Use a transition word for each step (see Focus on Reading, page 124).
- Finish the process with a transition word that shows the end of the process or the solution to the problem.
- Add any other necessary information.

B. Refer to Focus on Writing (page 133) or to the Models Chapter (page 169) to see an example of a process paragraph and to learn more about how to write one.

C. You received feedback on your Warm-Up Assignment from your teacher and classmates. Use this feedback to consider how you can improve your writing.

D. Proofread your paragraph. Check your spelling, grammar, and punctuation. Did you use transition words correctly?

E. Read your paragraph aloud. Are there any other errors? Make corrections and write a final copy. Share your paragraph with a partner.

My eLab ✎
Visit My eLab to build on what you learned.

How confident
are you?

Think about what you learned in this chapter. Use the table to decide what you should review. Share your answers with a partner.

I LEARNED ...	I AM CONFIDENT	I NEED TO REVIEW
vocabulary related to robots and artificial intelligence;	☐	☐
to recognize a process in a text;	☐	☐
to identify problems and solutions;	☐	☐
to use prepositions of time;	☐	☐
to describe a process;	☐	☐
how to study smarter;	☐	☐
how to write steps in a process and a process paragraph.	☐	☐

CHAPTER 8
Look Into the Future

What's next? You probably ask yourself about what will happen in the next few days, the next few years, and even hundreds of years in the future. Will the world be over-populated and poor? Or will it be filled with wonderful new technologies that take care of our needs for food, clothing, and shelter? Imagining the future is the first step to making it happen. What do you think the future will be like?

In this chapter,
you will

- learn vocabulary related to the future;

- make inferences when you read;

- use headings to understand ideas;

- review the present perfect tense;

- learn how to write questions for a questionnaire;

- learn how to prepare for exams;

- write a short questionnaire and summarize the findings in a paragraph.

GEARING UP

A. Look at the photo and then give your opinions on life in the future.

A HUNDRED YEARS FROM NOW ...	YES	NO
1 People will mostly travel by large floating airships.	☐	☐
2 Cities will be large blocks of connected buildings.	☐	☐
3 There will be no natural green spaces.	☐	☐
4 Most people will not have windows in their homes or offices.	☐	☐

B. Discuss the statements and your answers, first with a partner, then in a group.

Below are the key words you will practise in this chapter. Check the words you understand and then underline the words you use.

These words are from the Longman Communication 3000 and the Academic Word List. See Appendix 1, page 172.

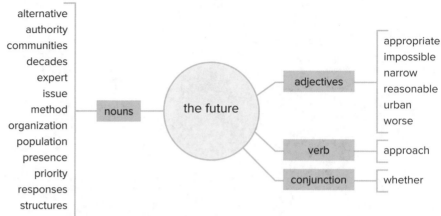

nouns:
alternative
authority
communities
decades
expert
issue
method
organization
population
presence
priority
responses
structures

the future

adjectives:
appropriate
impossible
narrow
reasonable
urban
worse

verb: approach

conjunction: whether

FOCUS ON READING

Making Inferences When You Read

Writers do not always complete an argument or offer a conclusion. Instead, they let you consider what you know and let you make a conclusion based on clues in the text. The conclusion you make is called an *inference*. Here are some ways to make inferences when you read.

• Ask yourself what you already know about the topic.

• Consider what the writer is *not* saying.

• While you read, look for clues in the text.

• Ask questions to reach a conclusion.

A. Read this excerpt from Reading 1. Then choose the best inference.

> Have you ever wondered if you could be an expert and predict the future? In 1977, when Ken Olson (1926–2011) was the head of the computer company Digital Equipment Corporation, he said, "There is no reason for any individual to have a computer in his home."

☐ You could be an expert and predict things.

☐ It's easy for anyone to predict the future.

☐ Experts can't always predict the future.

B. Here are four sentences from Reading 3. Choose the best inference for each sentence.

① One hundred years from now, the human population will be living in underwater cities.

    a) The population will be too large to build homes for everyone on land.

    b) Most people will have to learn to swim to get around in their city.

② Preparing food will become even easier, as recipes will be downloaded and 3D-printed, ready to eat within minutes.

    a) People will eat at restaurants more.

    b) People will eat at home more.

3 Floating communities will mean people can continuously move around to take advantage of the best climates.

   a) People will choose to be near major cities.

   b) People will choose warmer, sunnier places.

4 For those wanting to travel between these new "mega buildings," a new kind of drone-car will fly people directly.

   a) It will be difficult to reach parts of mega buildings without drone-cars.

   b) Most people will still drive cars and take elevators to reach mega buildings.

FOCUS ON CRITICAL THINKING

Using Headings to Understand Ideas

Titles and headings help you understand ideas. Headings break a longer text into smaller sections that have the same main idea. A heading makes it easier to predict what a section will be about.

A. Here is the title and the headings from Reading 1. What do you think the text will be about? Discuss with a partner.

TITLE: Predicting the Future
   HEADING 1: What do the experts know?
   HEADING 2: The trouble with pretending
   HEADING 3: Moving to Mars?

B. Read this excerpt from Reading 3. Underline the most important points and then write a heading.

> Buildings and interiors will evolve into flexible spaces, with rooms able to change size and shape depending on how many people are in there at one time. Walls, ceilings, and floors will have technology that will allow the bedroom to become much smaller and the living room larger when having guests over, for example.
>
> Homes will be controlled through software that will learn our living patterns and suggest appropriate decoration and furnishings, which will then be 3D-printed, according to Britain's leading space scientist, Dr. Maggie Aderin-Pocock.

HEADING: _____

 **READING ❶**   ## Predicting the Future

Before computers, it was nearly impossible to predict what life would be like in the 21st century. Mobile phones, digital watches and cameras, and driverless cars were all hard to imagine. But this did not stop experts from trying to guess the future. What do you think life will be like in a hundred years from now?

In the following exercises, explore key words from Reading 1.

A. Choose the word that has the closest meaning to the word in bold.

1. Have you ever wondered if you could be an **expert**?

   a) professional   b) amateur   c) participant

2. This all might make you infer that a colony on Mars is **impossible**.

   a) reasonable   b) practical   c) unthinkable

3. Mars One, a Dutch **organization**, predicts they will build a Mars colony by 2030.

   a) individual   b) group   c) factory

4. He did not **approach** the issue in a scientific way.

   a) reject   b) explore   c) ignore

5. People believed him because he seemed like an **authority**.

   a) specialist   b) librarian   c) inventor

B. The word *issue* can be a noun or a verb and *narrow* can be a verb or an adjective. Fill in the blanks using *issue* or *narrow*. Then indicate whether each is used as a noun, a verb, or an adjective.

SENTENCES	NOUN	VERB	ADJECTIVE
❶ The main _____ is to decide who is an expert.			
❷ He has a _____ view about surveys.			
❸ We had to _____ a report on the questionnaire.			
❹ I can't decide if the _____ is important or not.			
❺ We have to _____ our search to save time.			
❻ The _____ building is the taller one.			

C. What do the words in bold mean to you? Complete the sentences.

1. Do you know an **expert**?

   An expert I know is _____

   _____

2. What is **impossible** for you to do?

   It's impossible for me to _____

   _____

③ Which **organization** would you like
to work for?

I'd like to work for _____

_____

_____

④ How do you **approach** a new topic
you want to learn?

I start by _____

_____

_____

⑤ Which **issue** in the news interests
you?

I'm interested in _____

_____

Before You Read

A. Inferences are important to understanding an author's opinion. Reading 1
includes a quote from Robert de Neufville. What inference can you make about
de Neufville's opinion of experts? Write it below.

> "If you want to be considered an expert in something, you don't have to
> demonstrate real expertise. What you have to do is show you fit in and get
> along. That's why it's not surprising our experts get things wrong. By and
> large the people who run our government and who shape our opinions are
> the popular kids, not the ones who ace [do well on] the real world's tests."

INFERENCE: _____

_____

B. In the novel *1984*, George Orwell (1903–1950) made unlikely predictions that
have come true, such as continuous wars and governments rewriting the news.
Write four things you think will be different in the future: two that will be better
and two that will be worse. Then discuss in a group.

BETTER: _____

_____

WORSE: _____

_____

While You Read

C. While you read, make inferences about the author's opinion on experts.
Underline phrases that will help you draw your inferences.

obsolete (adj.): no longer made or used

pretend (v.): act like something is true when it's not

bother (v.): take trouble to do something

ace (v.): do well on

What do experts know?

Have you ever wondered if you could be an expert and predict the future? In 1977, when Ken Olson (1926–2011) was the head of the computer company Digital Equipment Corporation, he said, "There is no reason for any individual to have a computer in his home."

Many experts have predicted the future but they have often been wrong. This is perhaps because experts have had a narrow view of the future. They look at what they have learned and what they have done in their own work. They don't think that their knowledge could become **obsolete**. They cannot imagine the future will be different.

The trouble with pretending

Another problem is that experts in one field often **pretend** to be experts in another. A famous example is Oxford professor Sir Erasmus Wilson (1809–1884). He was a surgeon, not a scientist, but in 1878 he commented on a new invention, electric lights, "When the Paris Exhibition closes, electric light will close with it and no more will be heard of it."

We know that this is absurd, but many people agreed with Wilson. It's not just that Wilson was wrong. More importantly, he was respected as a scientist but he gave an opinion about something that he did not understand. He did not **approach** the **issue** in a scientific way. He did not **bother** to do research. But people believed him because he seemed like an **authority**.

Robert de Neufville (2015) writes,

> If you want to be considered an expert in something, you don't have to demonstrate real expertise. What you have to do is show you fit in and get along. That's why it's not surprising our experts get things wrong. By and large the people who run our government and who shape our opinions are the popular kids, not the ones who **ace** the real world's tests (para. 5).

Moving to Mars?

De Neufville's point is that we cannot trust experts. We have to question everything. We have to look at the data and make inferences. Give it a try by answering this question: Will people live on Mars? Mars One, a Dutch **organization** predicts they will build a Mars colony by 2030. Do you think this is possible?

But before you answer, consider data about costs and living conditions. The current cost of sending a kilo of weight to the International Space Station is between US $1,700 and US $20,200 (Johnson, 2015). The distance to the Space Station is a few hours; to Mars it is 150 to 300 days. People eat, on average, 1.5 to 2 kilos of food a day and

buried (v.): put underground

drink .9 kilos of water. But, currently, nothing can grow on Mars and there is no water that is not frozen and **buried**. You cannot breathe the air and the average temperature
45 is –60°C. This all might make you infer that a colony on Mars is **impossible**.

But perhaps the bigger question is, "Will people want to live on Mars?"   (486 words)

References

de Neufville, R. (2015). Why the experts get everything wrong. *Big Think*. Retrieved from http://bigthink.com/politeia/why-the-experts-get-everything-wrong

Johnson, E. (2015, November 27). Rockets: What is the cost of sending 1 kg into space? *Quora*. Retrieved from https://www.quora.com/Rockets-What-is-cost-of-sending-1-kg-weight-into-space

After You Read

D. Choose the phrase that best completes each sentence, according to the text.

1. The phrase "experts have had a narrow view of the future" means _____.

   a) the future will not be as wide

   b) the past is easier to understand

   c) experts cannot think of new ideas

2. The sentence, "They don't think that their knowledge could become obsolete" means _____.

   a) their ideas will likely come true

   b) they have already become obsolete

   c) they are out of touch with reality

3. You can infer from the story about electric lights that _____.

   a) experts should keep to their own areas

   b) electric lights are likely to continue to change

   c) electric lights may become unpopular

4. Part of the challenge of living on Mars is _____.

   a) the cost per kilo to send basic items

   b) the number of astronauts who want to go

   c) the high temperatures on the surface of Mars

5. The author's opinion of experts is that they are _____.

   a) usually right

   b) sometimes right and sometimes wrong

   c) usually wrong

E. According to the text, and the inferences you made, do you think people will want to live on Mars? Why or why not?

_____

_____

FOCUS ON GRAMMAR

> The past participle of regular verbs is the same as the past tense "-ed" form.

My eLab 📂

See the Irregular Verbs List in My eLab Documents for irregular past participles.

My eLab ✏️

Visit My eLab to complete Grammar Review exercises for this chapter.

Present Perfect Tense

You use the present perfect tense for two reasons:

- actions that started in the past and continue in the present;
- actions that occurred at a time in the past that is not clear.

Example: The RAND Corporation **has solved** countless problems.
This means that the RAND Corporation solved many problems in the past and continues to solve problems.

- Form the present perfect tense with the simple present tense of *have* and the past participle of the main verb.

Example: Many experts **have predicted** the future but they **have been** wrong often. This means that experts continue to predict the future and that they were wrong in the past and continue to be wrong.

- Form present perfect questions by changing the word order. Put *have* or *has* at the beginning of the question.

Example: **Have** many experts **predicted** the future?

A. Fill in the blanks with the present perfect tense. Use *have* or *has* and the past participle of the verb in parentheses.

1. (wonder) _____ you ever _____ if you could be an expert and predict the future?

2. (use) Researchers _____ questionnaires to predict the future for decades.

3. (prove) The method _____ to be effective and is still used today.

4. (learn) They look at what they _____ and what they have done in their own work.

5. (fail) But, often, these interviews _____ because people don't have time to talk.

B. Complete this paragraph. Fill in the blanks with the simple past tense or the past perfect tense of the verbs in parentheses. Remember that you use the simple past for things that have finished in the past.

There (be) _____ wars for thousands of years but, in 1949,

George Orwell (write) _____ about the idea of "continuous war."

He (predict) _____ that governments would keep fighting for

economic and political reasons. Many governments (keep) _____

their popularity by starting wars and citizens (feel) _____ unable

to criticize them. Now things (change) _____, partly

because the government cannot control the news. Governments (think)

_____ that the Internet would help the military communicate

during wars, but people (use) _____ it to protest wars.

Question the Questionnaire

Companies collect data about your opinions and preferences. They do this to help market many products and services. Some of your data is collected from what you look at, do, or buy online. A more direct way to collect data is with a questionnaire.

VOCABULARY BUILD

In the following exercises, explore key words from Reading 2.

A. Match each word to its definition.

WORDS		DEFINITIONS
❶ alternative (n.)	_____	a) way of doing something
❷ decades (n.)	_____	b) another possibility
❸ method (n.)	_____	c) poorer quality
❹ reasonable (adj.)	_____	d) answers
❺ responses (n.)	_____	e) periods of ten years
❻ worse (adj.)	_____	f) based on good sense

B. *Whether* is a conjunction used when making a comparison or a choice. Read the following sentences and draw an arrow ↓ to indicate where *whether* should be placed in each sentence.

❶ She asked the alternative was better than what they had now .

❷ They wondered it would take decades to get people to Mars .

❸ Do you know this method is safe ?

❹ Decide it's reasonable to plan a new city or not .

C. What do the words in bold mean to you? Complete the sentences.

❶ What's your **method** for getting a good sleep?

My method is _____

❷ What's your **response** when someone asks to study with you?

I usually say _____

❸ What's a **reasonable** time to get up in the morning?

I get up at _____

❹ What's **worse** than forgetting to prepare for an exam?

Something worse _____

❺ What's an **alternative** to going to the gym for exercise?

An alternative is _____

Before You Read

A. Reading 2 includes some results from a questionnaire. But before you read, choose your answers to these questions.

1 Will technological changes lead to a future where people's lives are _____?

a) mostly better

b) mostly worse

c) don't know

2 If robots became primary caregivers for the elderly, would it be _____?

a) mostly better

b) mostly worse

c) don't know

3 Would you have a brain implant to improve memory and mental capacity (thinking)?

a) would do it   b) would not do it   c) don't know

4 Would you ride in a driverless car?

a) would do it   b) would not do it   c) don't know

5 Will computers create important works of art such as music, novels, movies, and paintings?

a) definitely happen

b) probably happen

c) probably not happen

d) definitely not happen

B. Use headings to help you understand a text. Here is the title and the headings from Reading 2. What inference can you make about the text? Write it below.

TITLE: Question the Questionnaires

HEADING 1: A method to predict the future
HEADING 2: The PIAL Project
HEADING 3: Should you believe it?

INFERENCE: _____

_____

_____

While You Read

C. While you read, take notes on inferences you can make about the results of the PIAL Project questions.

A method to predict the future

❶

Vocabulary Tip: The prefix "re-," as in "rethink," means to do something again. Look for other words with the prefix "re-" and see if they have similar meanings.

A think tank is a group of people paid to examine issues and solve problems. Among the most famous is the RAND Corporation. They have solved countless problems. In
5 the 1950s, they wanted to create a tool to predict the future and developed the Delphi Method.

The Delphi Method starts with a questionnaire to find out what a group of experts think. After, the experts receive **feedback** on the group's **responses**. The experts then rethink their answers. The method has proved to be effective and is still used today.

10 ## The PIAL Project

Researchers have used questionnaires to predict the future for **decades**. One example is the Pew Internet and American Life (PIAL) Project. In 2014, a survey asked several questions about the future. The first question was **whether** technological changes would lead to a future where people's
15 lives are mostly better or where people's lives are mostly **worse**. The results were as follows:

- mostly better   59 %
- mostly worse   30 %
20 - don't know   10 %
- refused to answer   1 %

Other questions asked for responses such as whether or not something would

25 - **definitely** happen;
- probably happen;
- probably not happen;
- definitely not happen.

For example, one question asked whether computers would create important works of
30 art such as music, novels, movies, or paintings. Sixteen percent said that would "definitely happen," and 35 percent said that would "probably happen." An **alternative** question would be to ask *when* something would happen and have people write in a date.

Another question was whether several things in the future would be a change for the better or a change for the worse. For example, only one-third thought it would be a
35 change for the better if robots became primary **caregivers** for the elderly. A slightly smaller percentage would get a brain **implant** to improve memory or mental capacity—the ability to think.

For some issues, such as riding in a driverless car, 48 percent said they "would do it," 50 percent said they "would not do it," and 2 percent said they "didn't know."

Should you believe it?

All the data seems **reasonable**, but it's important to question the questionnaires. For example, consider how a questionnaire collects data and how many people answer the questions.

Questionnaires and surveys can be conducted in one of four ways: by mail, online, 45 in person, or by phone. Each has advantages and disadvantages. You may think mail and online questionnaires are easy to ignore, but at least the respondent can find a convenient time to answer them.

Talking to people in person is more interactive—they can ask questions if they don't understand. But, often, these interviews have failed because people don't have time 50 to talk. In fact, many people refuse to answer any questions at all. So, although PIAL says it interviewed 1,001 people, it does not provide information about how many people refused to answer.

Also, people don't always tell the truth or the questions are **misleading**. Who knows? Maybe many of those people who haven't liked robot caregivers or driverless cars 55 might change their mind once they get a brain implant.

(496 words)

References

Helmer-Hirschberg, O. (1967). *Analysis of the future: The Delphi Method*. Santa Monica, CA: RAND Corporation. Retrieved from http://www.rand.org/pubs/papers/P3558.html

PEW Research Center. (2014, April 17). Future of technology: Survey questions. *PIAL*. Retrieved from http://www.pewinternet.org/files/2014/04/Future-of-Tech_SurveyQuestions.pdf

After You Read

D. Indicate whether these statements are true or false, according to the text.

STATEMENTS	TRUE	FALSE
❶ The Delphi Method uses experts to predict the future.		
❷ For decades, people have used questionnaires to predict the future.		
❸ When asked, most people thought the future would be worse.		
❹ Most people thought computers would create important works of art.		
❺ Most people thought robots would make good primary caregivers.		
❻ People don't answer questions because they don't have time.		
❼ The last paragraph suggests people may change their minds.		

E. In Before You Read, task A, you chose answers to the questions in the table on the next page. Now compare your answers to the answers given by the PIAL Project respondents. Are your answers similar or different? Discuss with a partner.

QUESTIONS	SIMILAR	DIFFERENT
1 Will technological changes lead to a future where people's lives are mostly better or mostly worse?		
2 If robots became primary caregivers for the elderly, would it be mostly better or mostly worse?		
3 Would you have a brain implant to improve memory and mental capacity (thinking)?		
4 Would you ride in a driverless car?		
5 Will computers create important works of art such as music, novels, movies, and paintings?		

F. Consider the notes you took while you read. What's your general inference about people's perceptions of the future? Discuss with a partner.

FOCUS ON WRITING

Writing a Questionnaire

You ask questions constantly, such as, "What time is it?" Many questions have simple answers. For more complicated topics, use a questionnaire to collect the opinions of many people. Use online questionnaires to collect data from hundreds or thousands of people.

Learning to write a questionnaire is a useful skill and it helps you to better understand questionnaires that you might need to answer. It is also important to know how to analyze a questionnaire's answers and write about the findings.

Writing a questionnaire starts with a topic you want to have more information about. Sometimes you collect general information to learn more about the participants, such as their age range, education, and occupation. These are followed by factual questions (Have you been to Antarctica?), and opinion questions (What do you think about living on Mars?). The questions should be simple and easy to understand. Write as if you were talking to someone.

A. Write a general area you are interested in and a question for each type of information.

GENERAL AREA OF INTEREST: _____

_____

PERSONAL QUESTION: _____

FACTUAL QUESTION: _____

_____

OPINION QUESTION: _____

_____

Longer questionnaires often ask the same question in more than one way. It helps to check if answers are consistent.

B. Read these example questions. Each one has a problem when it comes to being used in a questionnaire. Match each question to its problem.

EXAMPLE QUESTIONS		PROBLEMS
❶ Many people think they would like to go to Mars and have put a lot of research into it and think it's a good idea. Do you agree?	_____	a) The question is too formal.
❷ Would you rather go to Mars or learn to explore caves?	_____	b) The question is too long.
❸ If one wishes to journey through space to Mars, how would one go about it?	_____	c) The question uses complex vocabulary.
❹ Would you brave Mars' pernicious effects of truncated access to oxygen?	_____	d) The question does not have one clear choice.
❺ Would you rather go to Mars or stay on Earth or decide later?	_____	e) The question is a mix of ideas.

❗ The words "survey" and "questionnaire" are often used to refer to the same thing. But, technically, a questionnaire is a written tool used in a survey.

WARM-UP ASSIGNMENT
Write a Short Questionnaire

Write a questionnaire to find out what your classmates think about the future.

A. Choose a topic from Reading 1 or Reading 2, for example, living on Mars. Write your topic in the table below.

B. Write five yes/no questions on your topic. Use a mix of factual and opinion questions (see Focus on Writing on the previous page). If your topic is living on Mars, you might ask:

• Have you ever considered becoming an astronaut? (factual)

• Do you think people will live on other planets some day? (opinion)

C. Use the present perfect tense (see Focus on Grammar, page 150) and verbs such as *considered, done, dreamed, imagined, learned, thought,* and *tried.* Refer to the Models Chapter (page 170) to see an example of a questionnaire and to learn more about how to write one.

MY TOPIC IS: _____	YES	NO
❶		
❷		
❸		
❹		
❺		

Use feedback from your teacher and classmates on this Warm-Up Assignment to improve your writing.

D. Check your spelling, grammar, and punctuation. Did you use the present perfect tense correctly?

E. Read your questions aloud. Are there any other errors? Make corrections and write your final copy.

F. Ask your questions to five classmates and record their answers in the *yes* or *no* columns.

 **READING ③**

Humans Will Live Underwater in a Hundred Years' Time

In 1800, the world's population reached one billion. By 2050, the United Nations expects it to reach 9.7 billion. One of the greatest challenges will be to find places for all those people to live. One possibility is underwater. After all, 71 percent of the Earth is covered in water. Would you like to live under the sea?

VOCABULARY BUILD

In the following exercises, explore key words from Reading 3.

A. Match each word to its antonym (word with the opposite meaning).

WORDS		ANTONYMS
❶ appropriate (adj.)	_____	a) absence
❷ presence (n.)	_____	b) unsuitable
❸ priority (n.)	_____	c) country
❹ urban (adj.)	_____	d) last choice

B. Fill in the blanks with the correct words to complete the sentences. Use each word twice.

communities	population	structures

❶ _____ are made up of different kinds of people.

❷ Creatures like birds and ants build complex _____ to live in.

❸ New _____ are possible with better building materials.

❹ The _____ of the moon is currently zero.

❺ Two _____ I have belonged to are in Beijing and Abu Dhabi.

❻ When a _____ is under threat by bad climate, it tends to move.

C. What do the words in bold mean to you? Complete the sentences.

❶ What's an **appropriate** way to thank a good friend?

I thank a friend by _____

My eLab ✎

Visit My eLab to complete
Vocabulary Review exercises
for this chapter.

2 Would you rather live in an **urban** area or outside a city?

I'd rather live _____

3 What's a **priority** for you every day?

A priority for me is _____

4 Which **community** or other group do you belong to?

I belong to _____

Before You Read

A. Reading 3 suggests that people may have to live underground in the future. Look at this picture of Melbourne, Australia. Write five things you might miss if you lived underground.

• _____

• _____

• _____

• _____

• _____

B. Besides living underground, the text predicts other things will happen in the next hundred years. Indicate what you think will happen or won't happen. Then discuss your answers in a group.

IN THE NEXT HUNDRED YEARS PEOPLE WILL HAVE ...	WILL HAPPEN	WON'T HAPPEN
1 homes with flexible rooms that change size.		
2 software that learns our living patterns and suggests decoration and furnishings.		
3 recipes that are downloaded and 3D-printed, ready to eat within minutes.		
4 underwater neighbourhoods.		
5 drone-cars to fly people between buildings.		
6 communities established on Mars and on the moon.		

While You Read

C. While you read, underline the main points in the paragraphs and then write headings. Remember a heading can be a short phrase or a question.

Humans Will Live Underwater in a Hundred Years' Time

Heading: _____

continuously (adv.): without interruption

One hundred years from now, the human **population** will be living in underwater cities and in 3D-printed homes, according to a study that looks at the future of living.

5 Buildings and interiors will evolve into flexible spaces, with rooms able to change size and shape depending on how many people are in there at one time. Walls, ceilings, and floors will have technology that will allow the bedroom to become much smaller and the living room larger when having guests over, for example.

Heading: _____

10 Homes will be controlled through software that will learn our living patterns and suggest **appropriate** decoration and furnishings, which will then be 3D-printed, according to Britain's leading space scientist, Dr. Maggie Aderin-Pocock.

Preparing food will become even easier, as recipes will be downloaded and 3D-printed, ready to eat within minutes.

15 **Heading:** _____

In a century's time, we'll be living underwater because land space in **urban** areas will be in short supply. Underwater neighbourhoods and floating **communities** will spring up, while building deeper into the earth will also become a **priority**.

Floating communities will mean people can **continuously** move around to take
20 advantage of the best climates.

Heading: _____

"Earth-Scrapers"—multi-level, **subterranean structures** that are built deep into the ground—will become popular places to live. The rise in "super basements" in London is an early example of people looking for more creative ways to add space in popular
25 cities.

Meanwhile, skyscrapers will reach **unprecedented** heights, and be able to host a whole town high above ground.

Prefabricated houses will be assembled on top of the buildings, connected by giant aerial highways and elevated **pedestrian** streets, with shopping outlets, cafes, and parks.

30 For those wanting to travel between these new "mega buildings," a new kind of drone-car will fly people directly.

Heading: _____

Today's rigid working week will also transform. More and more people will work from home, thanks to technological developments. This will include the use of holograms
35 to create a realistic 3D image that will beam into the home and remove the need for an actual presence in group meetings.

Digital developments in healthcare will also mean fewer visits to the doctor. Homes will be equipped with a step-in capsule, which will scan bodies and provide a diagnosis digitally.

40 A connected machine will then dispense treatment in the form of a pill, patch or jab—either within the home or outside in the neighbourhood.

Heading: _____

Finally, space flights will become commonplace and there will also be communities established on Mars and the moon.

45 People looking to unwind will be able to take virtual holidays, through a sophisticated headset that generates the sounds, the sense of movement, and even the smells of a holiday resort or popular travel destination.

(448 words)

Anderson, E. (2016, February 15). Humans will live underwater in 100 years' time as the population is squeezed out of cities. *The Telegraph*. Retrieved from http://www.telegraph.co.uk/finance/newsbysector/constructionand property/12157503/Humans-will-live-underwater-in-100-years-time-as-the-population-is-squeezed-out-of-cities.html

After You Read

D. Review the headings you wrote in the text. Discuss them with a partner. How are they similar? How are they different?

E. Choose the phrase that best completes each sentence, according to the text.

1. Flexible space will allow rooms to hold different _____.
   a) numbers of people
   b) kinds of furniture
   c) kitchens and bedrooms

2. Instead of buying furniture at a store, you will _____.
   a) order it online
   b) mostly sit on the floor
   c) have it 3D-printed

3. The term "earth-scraper" was probably invented because people _____.
   a) won't live in a hole
   b) understand skyscrapers
   c) will have to dig to live

4. The buildings that will reach unprecedented heights will be for _____.
   a) more people to live in
   b) offices for meetings
   c) more rooftop gardens

5. The importance of holograms is to allow people to _____.
   a) work for less money
   b) work more from home
   c) have larger offices

6. Virtual holidays will be different because you will also get _____.
   a) to meet other people
   b) the taste of food
   c) the smells of a place

F. The reading predicts a number of things that will happen in the next hundred years. Choose one and explain why you think it will happen or will not happen.

_____

_____

_____

Academic
Survival Skill

Preparing for Exams

In Chapter 7, you learned ways to study smarter. Once you have good studying skills, you then need to consider how to improve your exam skills. When you are prepared for exams, you will do better on them.

▶

A. Following are seven strategies that can improve your exam performance. Indicate which strategies you already do and which you should do.

EXAM STRATEGIES		ALREADY DO	SHOULD DO
BEFORE THE EXAM	a) Find out as much as possible about the exam. Ask your teacher and other students. Is there a practice exam or an example from last year?		
	b) Get enough sleep before the exam. It's better to get up early than to stay up all night.		
DURING THE EXAM	c) Make sure you have all the materials you need (e.g., things to write with, a dictionary, if allowed). Check the time you have and bring a watch or clock to make sure you use your time efficiently.		
	d) Read the questions carefully. Underline the important parts in each one. Some students miss important details or write too much or too little.		
	e) Write an outline of your answers, especially for paragraph or essay questions. Check your outline before, while, and after you write.		
	f) Check your answers again and again. Don't leave early; leave when the exam is over. One mistake can be the difference between passing or failing.		
AFTER THE EXAM	g) Reflect on your exam. Consider what you did well and what you could improve on for next time. Ask for help from your teacher or other students.		

B. Read these problems. Write the letter of each strategy you should have used.

_____ I left early. I didn't realize there was another question on the last page.

_____ I was worried about the time so I just started writing the essay as quickly as possible.

_____ The content of the exam was totally unexpected. I studied all the wrong things.

_____ No wonder I failed. I guess I didn't really understand the question. It was too tricky.

_____ I would have done better if I checked my spelling and grammar. I thought it was perfect.

_____ The reason I ran out of time was my stupid pen—I only brought one and it broke.

_____ I should have passed. I studied until three in the morning for a whole week!

FINAL ASSIGNMENT

Write About Your Findings

The results of a questionnaire are called *findings*. Use what you learned in this chapter to write the findings of your Warm-Up Assignment questionnaire in a paragraph.

A. Organize the information from your questionnaire. Take notes below.

NOTES		EXPLANATIONS
TOPIC SENTENCE	Five students were asked ...	*Write the topic of your questionnaire as the opening sentence.*
FINDINGS	All of the students said ... Three of five of the students said ... None of the students said ...	*Summarize the responses to three of the five questions. Write sentences that explain the responses. When you write a number at the start of a sentence, write it as a word.*
CONCLUSION	Based on the results I can infer ...	*What can you infer from the findings? Conclude with a comment about the overall results.*

B. Write a draft of your paragraph. Use the present perfect tense where possible (see Focus on Grammar, page 150). Refer to the Models Chapter (page 171) to see an example of how to write the findings of a questionnaire in a paragraph.

C. Proofread your paragraph. Check your spelling, grammar, and punctuation. Did you use the present perfect tense correctly?

D. Read your paragraph aloud. Are there any other errors? Make corrections and write a final copy. Write a title for your paragraph and then share it with a partner.

How confident are you?

Think about what you learned in this chapter. Use the table to decide what you should review. Share your answers with a partner.

I LEARNED ...	I AM CONFIDENT	I NEED TO REVIEW
vocabulary related to the future;	☐	☐
to make inferences when reading a text;	☐	☐
to use headings to understand ideas;	☐	☐
the present perfect tense;	☐	☐
to write questions for a questionnaire;	☐	☐
how to prepare for exams;	☐	☐
how to write a short questionnaire and summarize the findings in a paragraph.	☐	☐

My eLab ✎

Visit My eLab to build on what you learned.

MODELS CHAPTER

This chapter provides models for the writing assignments found in *LEAP 1: Reading and Writing*. All are based on ideas about travel. Using travel as a common topic lets you see how similar information can be organized for different writing assignments.

Before each model, **you will find**

- instructions that highlight the key characteristics of the writing assignment;
- if applicable, the plan that the writer used to prepare for the writing assignment.

MODEL 1 **How to Write Lists**

Lists are used for different purposes. They can help you organize your thoughts and ideas. You can make notes on things you need to do. Use a list to break down a complicated topic or task into smaller parts or steps. You can also use a list to remember a sequence of events. Lists are easy to write and easy to read.

Instructions

- Write the topic or subject of your list as a heading or title.
- Choose the format that works best for your topic: bullet points or numbers.
- Brainstorm ideas, items, steps, or events relevant to your topic. Write simple sentences.
- Highlight what is important and prioritize. Decide what comes first, what comes next, what comes last.
- Organize your list.
- Check your grammar and spelling.
- Make corrections and write a final copy.

Example 1: List of Goals

Write a list of travel goals.

The title is optional.

The list starts with the main goal, then lists other places in Australia that are important, and ends with places and things that would be nice to visit if possible.

List of Travel Goals

• I have to travel to Australia.

• I can visit Sydney and Melbourne.

• I should visit Tasmania.

• I could see the Barrier Reef and Uluru.

The modals show how necessary or possible it is to visit each place.

Example 2: Chronological List

Write a list of early events in Machu Picchu.

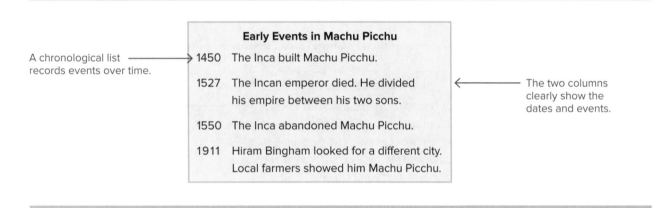

A chronological list records events over time.

Early Events in Machu Picchu

1450	The Inca built Machu Picchu.
1527	The Incan emperor died. He divided his empire between his two sons.
1550	The Inca abandoned Machu Picchu.
1911	Hiram Bingham looked for a different city. Local farmers showed him Machu Picchu.

The two columns clearly show the dates and events.

MODEL 2 How to Write a Paragraph

A paragraph is a group of connected sentences on the same topic. A paragraph includes a topic sentence, supporting sentences, and a concluding sentence.

Instructions

• Write a topic sentence to suggest the reason you are writing. The topic sentence explains your main idea, but doesn't give detailed information.

• Add supporting sentences that expand on the idea or ideas of your topic sentence. These might include examples and explanations.

• End with a conclusion that says something new.

• Write the topic or subject of your paragraph as a heading or title.

Example 1: Descriptive Paragraph

Describe your travel goals.

The title is a simple summary.

> **My Travel Goals**
>
> My goal is to travel to Australia. I can visit Sydney, Melbourne, and other cities. I should visit Tasmania too. I could scuba dive at the Great Barrier Reef. I could see Uluru, a large sandstone rock, at sunset. I have to travel to Australia soon.

The topic sentence gives the main idea.

Supporting sentences expand on the main idea with examples and explanations.

The paragraph ends with a conclusion that says something new.

Example 2: Chronological Paragraph

Describe early events in Machu Picchu.

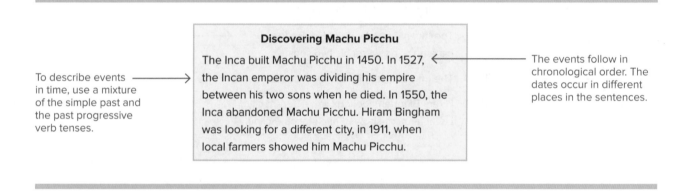

To describe events in time, use a mixture of the simple past and the past progressive verb tenses.

> **Discovering Machu Picchu**
>
> The Inca built Machu Picchu in 1450. In 1527, the Incan emperor was dividing his empire between his two sons when he died. In 1550, the Inca abandoned Machu Picchu. Hiram Bingham was looking for a different city, in 1911, when local farmers showed him Machu Picchu.

The events follow in chronological order. The dates occur in different places in the sentences.

MODEL 3   How to Write a Formal Email

A formal email shares or asks for information from someone who is not a close friend or family member. Typically, formal emails are used in business to exchange information. It is important to be polite in a formal email.

Instructions

- In the *To:* line, write the person's email address.
- In the *Subject:* line, briefly explain why you are writing.
- In the body of the email, include a proper greeting such as *Dear* along with: *Ms., Mrs., Mr.,* or *Dr.,* and the person's last name followed with a comma.
- Give an introduction to explain why you are writing.
- End with *Yours sincerely,* or *Sincerely.* Include your first and last name and, if necessary, something else to identify you, such as your role as a student in a course.

Example of a Formal Email

Write a formal email to request permission.

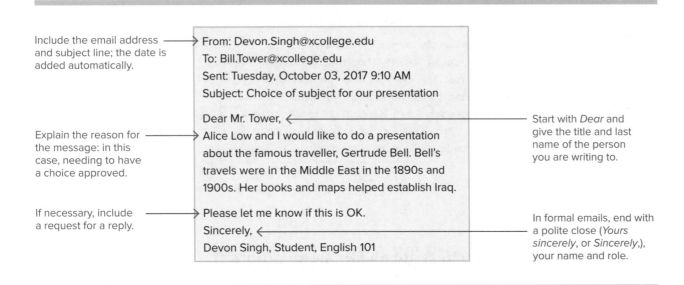

Include the email address and subject line; the date is added automatically.

From: Devon.Singh@xcollege.edu
To: Bill.Tower@xcollege.edu
Sent: Tuesday, October 03, 2017 9:10 AM
Subject: Choice of subject for our presentation

Dear Mr. Tower,

Start with *Dear* and give the title and last name of the person you are writing to.

Explain the reason for the message: in this case, needing to have a choice approved.

Alice Low and I would like to do a presentation about the famous traveller, Gertrude Bell. Bell's travels were in the Middle East in the 1890s and 1900s. Her books and maps helped establish Iraq.

If necessary, include a request for a reply.

Please let me know if this is OK.
Sincerely,
Devon Singh, Student, English 101

In formal emails, end with a polite close (*Yours sincerely*, or *Sincerely*,), your name and role.

MODEL 4   How to Write a Comparison Paragraph

A comparison paragraph shows similarities between two or more people, places, things, or ideas. Comparison paragraphs are often used to support an argument or proposal.

Instructions

- Decide which method of organization you will use: the point-by-point method or the block method.
- Write a topic sentence that identifies the two things you are comparing. Note: you can compare more than two things.
- Write three or more points of comparison that show similarities.
- Write a conclusion.

Example 1: Point-by-point Method

Compare two cities.

The title identifies what is being compared.

Tokyo and Beijing Will Host the Olympics

Tokyo and Beijing are both capital cities in Asia. Tokyo is the largest city in Japan. Beijing is not the largest city in China, but it is larger than Tokyo. Both cities are going to host the Olympics. Tokyo will host the 2020 Summer Olympics and Beijing is going to host the 2022 Winter Olympics. Large Asian cities are popular locations for the Olympics.

Comparatives and superlatives give information about the two cities.

There are differences but the similarities are more important in a comparison paragraph.

The comparisons start with what the cities have in common.

Both *be going to* and *will* are used to talk about the future.

The conclusion says something new.

Example 2: Block Method

The title identifies what is being compared. →

Tokyo and Beijing Will Host the Olympics

The Asian city Tokyo is the capital and largest city in Japan. Tokyo will host the 2020 Summer Olympics. The Asian city Beijing is the capital city of China. It's not the largest city in China, but it is larger than Tokyo. Beijing is going to host the 2022 Winter Olympics. Large Asian cities are popular locations for the Olympics.

Comparatives and superlatives give information about the cities. →

← Each city is described separately.

← Both *be going to* and *will* are used to talk about the future.

MODEL 5 | How to Write an Opinion Paragraph

An opinion paragraph offers opinions, but supports them with facts to form a reasonable argument with valid opinions.

Instructions

- Consider a topic or issue and decide on your opinions about it.
- Look for facts that support your opinion, to form valid opinions.
- Write a topic sentence that introduces the main idea and gives your opinion about it.
- Write supporting sentences. Use facts and valid opinions.
- Write a concluding sentence that says something new.
- Write a title that attracts attention.

Example of an Opinion Paragraph

What is the world's most popular city?

WRITER'S PLAN	
IDENTIFY A TOPIC OR ISSUE	• the most popular city in the world
WRITE A TOPIC SENTENCE	• opinion: Hong Kong most popular with visitors
WRITE SUPPORTING SENTENCES	• valid opinions and facts why Hong Kong is popular • statistics from market researcher Euromonitor International
WRITE A CONCLUDING SENTENCE	• needs more ways to stay popular
WRITE A TITLE	Hong Kong: The World's Most Popular City

Hong Kong: The World's Most Popular City

The topic sentence states an opinion; readers will look for supporting facts.

Hong Kong is the world's most popular city in terms of visitors. In 2015, 59.3 million people visited Hong Kong. In fact, it had more visitors from 2008 to 2015 than any other city in the world, according to market researcher Euromonitor International. More people go to Hong Kong than any other city because it is an exciting place with great food and shopping. However, to remain popular, Hong Kong needs to find more ways to attract visitors.

Statistics support the title, but readers might question if *most visitors equals most popular*.

The conclusion suggests an action Hong Kong should take to remain popular.

MODEL 6   How to Write a Process Paragraph

A process paragraph explains how something is done, or how something happened, or will happen.

Instructions

- Start with a topic sentence that includes a problem.
- Explain terms the reader might not know.
- Use prepositions of time to show when things happen.
- Use a transition word for each step. These include words like *to begin* and *finally* as well as ordinal numbers (e.g., *first, second, third*).
- Add any other necessary information to help explain your topic.
- Finish the process with a transition word that shows the end of the process or the solution to the problem.
- Choose a title that makes it clear what the process is.

Example of a Process Paragraph

Write the steps for checking into a hotel.

The word *steps* in the title suggests this is a process.

Numbered steps make the ideas in the paragraph easy to follow.

Steps for Checking into a Hotel

Checking into a hotel is not always a smooth process. First, check to see if you are at the right hotel. Hotels can have more than one location in the same city. Second, have your reservation information. Third, present identification and a credit card when you check in. Fourth, check to see the room is the same as the one you reserved: for example, the correct number of beds. Finally, ask for a key card for each person checking in. Follow these simple steps and your hotel stay will be more relaxed.

The topic sentence outlines the problem.

The word *finally* shows the end of the process.

The conclusion says something new.

MODEL 7.1 How to Write a Questionnaire

Use questionnaires to collect information. They follow a theme and the questions are related to each other. The questions and answer choices need to be clear and concise so the person answering completely understands them.

Instructions

- Choose a topic that you want to have more information about.
- Explain anything that might be unclear to people answering the questionnaire.
- Write questions with a common answer format: yes/no, true/false, or numbered choices.
- The questions can ask for factual information, opinions, or a mix of the two.
- Be sure to thank the respondent in person or in writing if the questionnaire is not given in person.
- Write a title so people know what the questionnaire is about.

Example of a Questionnaire

Write a short questionnaire about travel by Hyperloop.

WRITER'S PLAN	
CHOOSE A TOPIC	• people's interest in travelling by Hyperloop
EXPLAIN IF NECESSARY	• Hyperloop will connect Los Angeles with San Francisco and travel at speeds of up to 1,200 kilometres an hour.
WRITE YES/NO QUESTIONS	• travel by train/plane more than once a year? • heard of Hyperloop? • take a trip on one? • price?
WRITE A TITLE	• Hyperloop Questionnaire

The title identifies that this is a questionnaire.

The answers all follow one format with *yes/no* answer options.

Add a *thank you* when the questionnaire is conducted by mail or electronically.

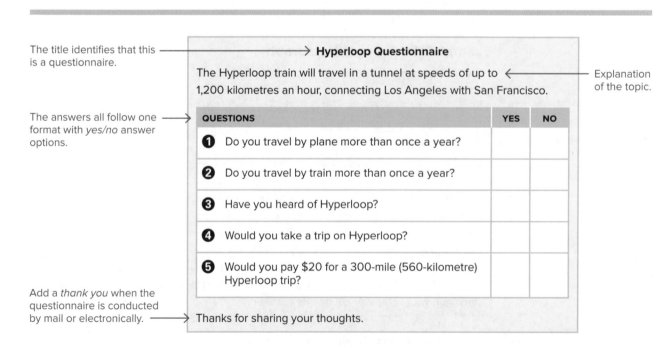

Hyperloop Questionnaire

The Hyperloop train will travel in a tunnel at speeds of up to 1,200 kilometres an hour, connecting Los Angeles with San Francisco.

Explanation of the topic.

QUESTIONS	YES	NO
❶ Do you travel by plane more than once a year?		
❷ Do you travel by train more than once a year?		
❸ Have you heard of Hyperloop?		
❹ Would you take a trip on Hyperloop?		
❺ Would you pay $20 for a 300-mile (560-kilometre) Hyperloop trip?		

Thanks for sharing your thoughts.

MODEL 7.2   How to Write the Findings of a Questionnaire

Findings are the answers people (respondents) give to a questionnaire.
After all the questionnaires are completed, collect them and add up the totals.
You need to examine the findings to draw inferences about what they mean.

Instructions

- Write the topic of your questionnaire as the opening sentence.
- Summarize the responses to the questions. Note: you may choose to ignore some questions and focus on the ones that are of most interest.
- Write sentences that explain the responses.
- Write about what you can infer from the findings.
- Conclude with a comment about the overall results.
- Write a sentence that says what is most important about your questionnaire.

Example of a Paragraph about the Findings of a Questionnaire

Write the findings of the Hyperloop questionnaire.

The title relates to the inference in the conclusion.

The topic sentence explains the questionnaire, including the number of people who responded.

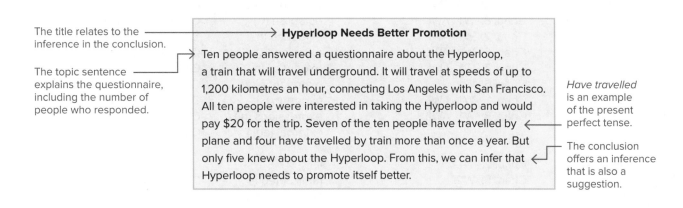

Hyperloop Needs Better Promotion

Ten people answered a questionnaire about the Hyperloop, a train that will travel underground. It will travel at speeds of up to 1,200 kilometres an hour, connecting Los Angeles with San Francisco. All ten people were interested in taking the Hyperloop and would pay $20 for the trip. Seven of the ten people have travelled by plane and four have travelled by train more than once a year. But only five knew about the Hyperloop. From this, we can infer that Hyperloop needs to promote itself better.

Have travelled is an example of the present perfect tense.

The conclusion offers an inference that is also a suggestion.

APPENDIX 1 Vocabulary

W1: one of the 1000 most frequent words in written English
W2: one of the next 1000 most frequent words (1000–2000)
W3: one of the next 1000 most frequent words (2000–3000)
AWL: on the Academic Word List

A

abandon (v.)	Chap. 3: W3 AWL
abilities (n.)	Chap. 7: W1
access (n.)	Chap. 4: W1 AWL
accounted (v.)	Chap. 6: W2
achieve (v.)	Chap. 1: W1 AWL
acquired (v.)	Chap. 6: W2 AWL
active (adj.)	Chap. 2: W2
advantages (n.)	Chap. 4: W1 AWL
advice (n.)	Chap. 1: W2
alternative (n.)	Chap. 8: W3 AWL
annual (adj.)	Chap. 3: W2 AWL
applied (v.)	Chap. 2: W1 AWL
appreciate (v.)	Chap. 4: W3 AWL
approach (v.)	Chap. 8: W2 AWL
appropriate (adj.)	Chap. 8: W1 AWL
aspect (n.)	Chap. 2: W1 AWL
assume (v.)	Chap. 6: W1 AWL
assumed (v.)	Chap. 7: W1 AWL
attention (n.)	Chap. 6: W1
attitudes (n.)	Chap. 1: W1 AWL
authority (n.)	Chap. 8: W1 AWL

B

behaviours (n.)	Chap. 2: W1
budget (n.)	Chap. 5: W2

C

campaigns (n.)	Chap. 5: W1
certain (adj.)	Chap. 4: W1
challenges (n.)	Chap. 1: W2 AWL
character (n.)	Chap. 6: W1
charge (v.)	Chap. 6: W2
commit (v.)	Chap. 6: W2 AWL
common (adj.)	Chap. 3: W1
communities (n.)	Chap. 8: W1 AWL
complex (adj.)	Chap. 3: W2 AWL
concentrating (v.)	Chap. 1: W2 AWL
confidence (n.)	Chap. 1: W2
consumers (n.)	Chap. 4: W2 AWL
context (n.)	Chap. 3: W2 AWL
contract (n.)	Chap. 3: W2 AWL
contributed (v.)	Chap. 3: W2 AWL
created (v.)	Chap. 2: W1 AWL
credit (n.)	Chap. 2: W2 AWL
crisis (n.)	Chap. 5: W2
criticized (v.)	Chap. 4: W3
cultures (n.)	Chap. 1: W1 AWL
cycle (n.)	Chap. 3: W3 AWL

D

decades (n.)	Chap. 8: W2 AWL
decision (n.)	Chap. 6: W1
decisions (n.)	Chap. 7: W1
depends (v.)	Chap. 5: W2
despite (prep.)	Chap. 3: W1 AWL
destroy (v.)	Chap. 2: W2
development (n.)	Chap. 4: W1 AWL
devices (n.)	Chap. 7: W2 AWL
disappear (v.)	Chap. 4: W2

E

efficient (adj.)	Chap. 1: W3
environment (n.)	Chap. 3: W1
environments (n.)	Chap. 7: W1 AWL
establish (v.)	Chap. 3: W1 AWL
evidence (n.)	Chap. 3: W1 AWL
examine (v.)	Chap. 6: W2
expenses (n.)	Chap. 5: W2
experience (v.)	Chap. 5: W2
expert (n.)	Chap. 8: W2 AWL
expressions (n.)	Chap. 7: W2
external (adj.)	Chap. 7: W2 AWL

F

familiar (adj.)	Chap. 1: W2
financial (adj.)	Chap. 2: W1 AWL

G

generate (v.)	Chap. 2: W2 AWL
generation (n.)	Chap. 2: W2 AWL

H

handling (v.)	Chap. 7: W2
happened (v.)	Chap. 4: W1

I

imagine (v.)	Chap. 5: W2
impact (n.)	Chap. 4: W2 AWL
implications (n.)	Chap. 2: W2 AWL
impossible (adj.)	Chap. 8: W2
improve (v.)	Chap. 5: W1
improvement (n.)	Chap. 2: W2
increasingly (adv.)	Chap. 4: W2
independence (n.)	Chap. 7: W2
industries (n.)	Chap. 4: W1 AWL
influence (n.)	Chap. 2: W1
injuries (n.)	Chap. 7: W2 AWL
instructions (n.)	Chap. 1: W2 AWL

internationally (adv.)   Chap. 3: W1
investments (n.)   Chap. 4: W1   AWL
involved (v.)   Chap. 6: W1
issue (n.)   Chap. 8: W1   AWL

L

launch (v.)   Chap. 2: W2
limit (n.)   Chap. 7: W2
linked (v.)   Chap. 2: W2   AWL

M

maintain (v.)   Chap. 5: W1   AWL
materials (n.)   Chap. 4: W1   AWL
measure (v.)   Chap. 5: W2
method (n.)   Chap. 8: W1   AWL
mission (n.)   Chap. 2: W2

N

narrow (adj.)   Chap. 8: W2
natural (adj.)   Chap. 6: W1
normally (adv.)   Chap. 6: W2   AWL

O

objects (n.)   Chap. 7: W2
operate (v.)   Chap. 7: W2
opportunities (n.)   Chap. 1: W1
options (n.)   Chap. 5: W2   AWL
organization (n.)   Chap. 8: W1
overestimate (v.)   Chap. 1: W2   AWL

P

particular (adj.)   Chap. 5: W1
percent (n.)   Chap. 1: W2   AWL
personal (adj.)   Chap. 5: W1
perspective (n.)   Chap. 4: W3   AWL
physical (adj.)   Chap. 7: W1   AWL
popularity (n.)   Chap. 4: W1   AWL
population (n.)   Chap. 8: W1
positive (adj.)   Chap. 2: W2   AWL
potential (adj.)   Chap. 4: W2   AWL
powerful (adj.)   Chap. 7: W2
precisely (adv.)   Chap. 6: W3   AWL
prepare (v.)   Chap. 5: W1
presence (n.)   Chap. 8: W2
principle (n.)   Chap. 7: W1   AWL
priority (n.)   Chap. 8: W2   AWL
private (adj.)   Chap. 5: W1
production (n.)   Chap. 4: W1   AWL
professional (adj.)   Chap. 3: W1   AWL
progress (n.)   Chap. 5: W2
properly (adv.)   Chap. 1: W2

R

raise (v.)   Chap. 6: W1
realize (v.)   Chap. 4: W1
reasonable (adj.)   Chap. 8: W2
reduce (v.)   Chap. 3: W1
refuse (v.)   Chap. 6: W1
rejected (v.)   Chap. 2: W2   AWL
relate (v.)   Chap. 6: W1
relationship (n.)   Chap. 2: W1
relevant (adj.)   Chap. 1: W2   AWL
repeat (v.)   Chap. 6: W2
responded (v.)   Chap. 3: W2   AWL
response (n.)   Chap. 7: W1   AWL
responses (n.)   Chap. 8: W1   AWL
revenue (n.)   Chap. 4: W2   AWL
rights (n.)   Chap. 3: W1
route (n.)   Chap. 7: W2   AWL
routine (n.)   Chap. 1: W3

S

satisfy (v.)   Chap. 5: W2
schedule (n.)   Chap. 1: W3   AWL
schedules (n.)   Chap. 3: W3   AWL
seeking (v.)   Chap. 6: W1
self-conscious (adj.)   Chap. 1: W3
separated (v.)   Chap. 6: W2
serious (adj.)   Chap. 6: W1
share (v.)   Chap. 3: W1
significant (adj.)   Chap. 2: W2   AWL
spread (v.)   Chap. 5: W2
strategic (adj.)   Chap. 1: W3   AWL
structures (n.)   Chap. 8: W2   AWL
support (v.)   Chap. 7: W2
surgery (n.)   Chap. 7: W2
survey (n.)   Chap. 1: W2
survive (v.)   Chap. 5: W2   AWL

T

term (n.)   Chap. 4: W1   AWL
traditional (adj.)   Chap. 3: W1   AWL

U

underestimate (v.)   Chap. 1: W2   AWL
unique (adj.)   Chap. 3: W2   AWL
urban (adj.)   Chap. 8: W2

V

variation (n.)   Chap. 6: W2   AWL
versions (n.)   Chap. 5: W2   AWL
virtual (adj.)   Chap. 5: W2   AWL
volumes (n.)   Chap. 7: W2   AWL

W

whether (conj.)   Chap. 8: W1
worrying (v.)   Chap. 2: W2
worse (adj.)   Chap. 8: W2

PHOTO CREDITS

ELECTROROBO.COM

pp. ix, 122, 141 © Benoît Lavoie.

FOTOLIA

pp. viii, 2, 21 © stokkete; p. 3 © ksuksu; p. 5 © bakharev; p. 6 © moccabunny; p. 7 © Andres Rodriguez; p. 8 (r) © Monkey Business; p. 8 (l) © BortN66; p. 11 © Creativa Images; p. 12 © ikop; p. 13 © Cybrain; p. 15 © sdecoret; p. 16 © pressmaster; p. 18 © Rawpixel.com; pp. viii, 22, 41 © MIMOHE; p. 23 © treenabeena; p. 24 (l) © Juulijs; p. 24 (c) © Leo Blanchette; p. 26 © milosljubicic; p. 27 © bogdandimages; p. 28 © StockPhotoPro; p. 30 © theromb; p. 31 (t,l) © savanno; p. 31 (t,r) © milanmarkovic78; p. 31 (b,l) © Panama; p. 31 (b,r) © gstockstudio; p. 33 © Sensay; p. 34 © slavun; p. 35 (l) © Image4pro; p. 35 (r) © joyfuji; p. 36 © javlindy; p. 37 (t) © Monkey Business; p. 37 (b) © MG; p. 38 © vectorfusionart; p. 39 © iko; p. 40 (t) © vlad_d; p. 40 (b) © CYCLONEPROJECT; p. 45 © Olexander; p. 46 © pummy; p. 48 © ketrin08; p. 49 © pfpgroup; p. 50 © kurapatka; p. 51 (t) © tab62; p. 51 (t,m) © WavebreakmediaMicro; p. 51 (b,m) © Nejron Photo; p. 51 (b) © SeanPavonePhoto; p. 54 © erika8213; p. 55 © weerasak; p. 57 © fuzzbones; p. 58 © Daniel Prudek; p. 60 (l) © mrcats; p. 60 (l,c) © Martinan; p. 60 (r,c) © WavebreakMediaMicro; p. 60 (r) © undrey; pp. viii, 62, 81 © ansyvan; p. 64 © kuznetsov_konsta; p. 65 © olegkruglyak3; p. 66 © jakkapan; p. 67 © Douglas Tomk; p. 68 © glisic_albina; p. 69 © Lee Brennan; p. 70 © donatas1205; p. 71 © michaeljung; p. 72 (t,l) © jolopes; p. 72 (t,r) © t0m15; p. 72 (m,l) © Oleksandr Delyk; p. 72 (m,c) © kmiragaya; p. 72 (m,r) © Juulijs; p. 72 (b) © Photographee.eu; p. 75 © psphotography; p. 76 © Rawpixel.com; p. 77 (t) © upslim; p. 77 (b) © mastock; p. 79 © bykobrinphoto; pp. viii, 82, 101 © tiero; p. 84 © BillionPhotos.com; p. 85 © Cifotart; p. 86 © dmitriisimakov; p. 87 © Audrey Popov; p. 88 © Artur Marciniec; p. 89 © Photocreo Bednarek; p. 90 © okanakdeniz; p. 92 © James Thew; p. 93 © julief514; p. 94 © Maridav; p. 98 © Maksim Šmeljov; p. 99 © vectorfusionart; p. 100 © Monkey Business; p. 103 © Family Business; p. 104 © olly; p. 106 © xy; p. 107 © iQoncept; p. 108 © tverdohlib; p. 110 © ramonespelt; p. 111 © YakobchukOlena; p. 112 © kantver; p. 114 © BillionPhotos.com; p. 116 © alphaspirit; p. 118 © Ekaterina Pokrovsky; p. 120 © goodman photo; p. 123 © Sergey Nivens; p. 125 (t) © geocislariu; p. 125 (b) © destina; p. 126 © imtmphoto; p. 127 © dmitrygolikov; p. 129 © ktsdesign; p. 130 © myvisuals; p. 131 © Frank; p. 132 (t) © weerapat1003; p. 132 (b) © ktsdesign; p. 134 © perfectmatch; p. 135 (t,l) © Normad_Soul; p. 135 (t,m) © Becker; p. 135 (t,r) © AltoClassic; p. 135 (b,l) © ZaZa studio; p. 135 (b,r) © JeKh; p. 137 (t,l) © naka; p. 137 (t,r) © Nataliya Hora; p. 137 (b,l) © yevgeniy11; p. 137 (b,r) © highwaystarz; p. 138 © science photo; p. 139 © GenuisMinus; p. 140 © Rido; pp. ix, 142, 163 © Kovalenko I; p. 143 © juanmrgt; p. 144 © isoga; p. 145 © Luca Oleastri; p. 146 © Luca Oleastri; p. 147 © zavgsg; p. 148 © Kovalenko I; p. 149 © Luca Oleastri; p. 150 © Dmitry Vereshchagin; p. 152 © Vladislav Kochelaevs; p. 153 © rolffimages; p. 155 © photology1971; p. 156 © Luca Oleastri; p. 158 © boyloso; p. 159 © Artur Marciniec; p. 160 © Luca Oleastri; p. 162 © WavebreakmediaMicro.

SHUTTERSTOCK

pp. viii, 42, 61 © Izf; p. 52 © JStone; pp. ix, 102, 121 © likebw.

WIKIMEDIA COMMONS

p. 25; p. 32; p. 47; p. 115.

TEXT CREDITS

CHAPTER 1

pp. 18–19 Excerpt from "How to study for an exam? Take a day off" by K. Houshmand © 2014 Kourosh Houshmand.

CHAPTER 2

pp. 37–38 Excerpt from "Meet the Canadian top 30 under 30" by Corporate Knights © 2015 Corporate Knights.

CHAPTER 3

p. 58 Excerpt from *Busy: How to thrive in a world of too much* by T. Crabbe © 2014, 2015 Tony Crabbe. Used by permission of Grand Central Publishing. All rights reserved.

CHAPTER 4

pp. 77–78 Excerpt from *Billionaires: Reflections on the upper crust* by D.M. West © 2014 The Brookings Institute.

CHAPTER 5

p. 98 Excerpt from "Three ways technology has changed our lives for the better" by Z. Morris © 2016 Zyana Morris.

CHAPTER 6

pp. 117–118 Excerpt from "Authors reveal 'Algorithms to Live By' " by J. Forani © 2016 *Toronto Star*/PARS.

CHAPTER 7

pp. 137–138 Excerpt from "Give us a hand: It's time for robots to get physical" by C. Thompson © 2016 Condé Nast.

CHAPTER 8

pp. 159–161 Excerpt from "Humans will live underwater in 100 years' time as the population is squeezed out of cities" by E. Anderson © 2016 *The Telegraph*.

NOTES